P9-BZQ-379

DATE DUE			
~~MAR 2 '77~~			
MAR 2 '77			
JUL 2 3 '77			
~~OC 29 '78~~			
~~MR 2 1 '84~~			
AP 1 8 '84			
APR 4 1984			
DE 2 '84			
NOV 2 7 1984			
MAR 7 '89			
FEB 2 8 '89			
RECEIVED			
APR 2 8 1999			
GAYLORD			PRINTED IN U.S.A.

PEACE IS NOT AT HAND

By the same Author

*

DEFEATING COMMUNIST INSURGENCY

REVOLUTIONARY WAR IN WORLD STRATEGY 1945-1969

NO EXIT FROM VIETNAM

PEACE IS
NOT AT HAND

By

Sir Robert Thompson

K.B.E., C.M.G., D.S.O., M.C.

David McKay Company, Inc.
New York

DS
558
T4.8
1974

PEACE IS NOT AT HAND

COPYRIGHT © 1974 BY SIR ROBERT THOMPSON

All rights reserved, including the right to reproduce this book, or parts thereof, in any form, except for the inclusion of brief quotations in a review.

First American Edition, 1974

LIBRARY OF CONGRESS CATALOG CARD NUMBER: 74-18614
MANUFACTURED IN THE UNITED STATES OF AMERICA
ISBN 0-679-50525-3

This book is dedicated
to the memory of

JOHN PAUL VANN,

Medal of Freedom,
a very brave man, a good friend,
a staunch ally and a great American.

'Without courage there can be no truth;
without truth there can be no other virtue.'
—Sir Walter Scott

395021

ALUMNI MEMORIAL LIBRARY
Creighton University
Omaha, Nebraska 68178

CONTENTS

vii

ACKNOWLEDGEMENTS

I am very grateful to all those who have encouraged me to write this book and who have assisted with suggestions, including the title. I would also like to thank all those who have helped with research and the checking of facts and figures. Figures can seldom be quite precise, but I have always taken the worst estimate, whether high or low, from the point of view of the argument. Any mistakes in these, and of course all opinions expressed, are entirely my own.

I am particularly grateful to Richard Natkiel F.R.G.S. who has provided me with the maps included in this volume.

Finally, I am greatly indebted to Miss Diana Keigwin, Mrs. Sarah Hicks and Miss Sarah Eden for so patiently taking dictation and typing the drafts and final typescript over the last year.

Robert Thompson
Winsford, Somerset
10 May, 1974

TERMS AND ABBREVIATIONS

ARVN   The Army of the Republic of Vietnam, i.e. South Vietnam's regular army, about 400,000 men.

B3 Front   This is the North Vietnamese term for the Central Highlands front opposite Kontum and Pleiku.

COSVN   The Central Office for South Vietnam. This is the headquarters for all NVA/VC operations in the southern part of South Vietnam, mainly Military Regions III and IV.

DRV   Democratic Republic of Vietnam. This is North Vietnam and I refer to its government in the text mainly as Hanoi.

GVN   The Government of the Republic of Vietnam, i.e. South Vietnam or Saigon.

ICC   The International Commission of Control, established by the Geneva Agreements of 1954 and operating in North and South Vietnam, Cambodia and Laos. Composed of Indians, Poles and Canadians.

ICCS   The International Commission of Control and Supervision, established by the Cease-fire Agreement of January, 1973, operating solely in South Vietnam, composed originally of Poles, Hungarians, Canadians and Indonesians. When the Canadians pulled out, they were replaced by Iranians.

Khmer Republic   The name given to Cambodia under its new constitution after 1970. The present government is known as the Government of the Khmer Republic (GKR).

KC
The Khmer Communists, sometimes called the Khmer Rouge, the name given to insurgent forces within Cambodia covering all three main factions.

Khmer Rouge
See above.

NLF
National Liberation Front. This was established by Hanoi in 1960 to give the Vietcong political representation at international level, and to maintain the fiction that the southern movement had a separate identity from the Indochina Communist Party and Hanoi.

NVA
The North Vietnamese regular army.

PF
Popular Forces. The full-time paid home guard of rifle platoons, each about 25–30 strong, with a total strength of about 250,000. They are normally recruited in, and serve in, their own villages.

POL
Petrol, oil, lubricants, or in American terms, mainly gasoline.

PRG
Provisional Revolutionary Government. This is the successor to the NLF and represents an elevation in status. It was one of the signatories of the Ceasefire Agreement.

PSDF
People's Self Defence Force, over 1·5 million strong with about 600,000 armed. These are part-time village militia defending their own hamlets.

Rangers, or
Ranger Groups
Ranger battalions are part of ARVN but can be separately allocated to Military Regions or Provinces. They are sometimes formed into regimental groups of three battalions.

RF
Paramilitary Regional Forces, normally recruited in and serving in their own provinces. Originally rifle companies, they were later formed into light infantry battalions and can now be used outside their own provinces. Total strength about 250,000.

RVNAF   Republic of Vietnam's Armed Forces.
             This term covers all forces and services—
             army, navy, air force, R F and P F.

VC   Vietcong. The name given to the successors
             of the Vietminh within South Vietnam of
             southern birth. The term has been used to
             differentiate between the insurgent move-
             ment within the South composed of
             southerners from North Vietnamese and
             North Vietnamese Army units.

Vietminh   The name given to the revolutionary
             movement established by the Indochina
             Communist Party (ICP), also known as
             the Lao Dong or Workers Party, in the
             war against the French from 1945 to 1954.

PREFACE

This has not been a pleasant book to write and it will not be a comfortable, or comforting, book to read, because it deals mainly with one of the most bitter wars in history and with the harsh reality of the danger which now faces the United States and the West.

It is because of that danger—that the United States may be preparing to acquiesce in their own strategic surrender—that I have felt compelled to write this book. But also, partly because I have been involved in the Vietnam war since 1961, I have felt it necessary to record, as I saw them, the events of that war from 1969 to the beginning of 1974 during the Nixon Administration. I fully appreciate that the people of the United States are weary of Vietnam and do not want to hear any more about it. Regrettably, however, it is not going to go away and this book, by explaining the events of the last few years, may help readers to understand future events in Vietnam and repercussions elsewhere. Finally, I have tried to put many controversial issues into perspective and I hope that this will help historians of the future, if only by indicating some of the areas where more objective research and analysis are required.

Two points have always impressed me with regard to the attitudes of American society, and that of the West generally, to the war. The first has been its abysmal ignorance of the nature and course of the war and of what was really happening behind the surface scenes which received so much publicity on television or in the press. I realize that there is so much else in American society to occupy the minds of its people and that the world outside receives scant attention. This is most noticeable in its major daily newspapers as compared, for example, with those in Europe. At the same time television has merely increased emotional feeling at the expense of intellectual judgement. It was not surprising that GIs looked forward to leaving 'the Nam' and getting back into the world. In fact what they meant was that they found the world unaccountably too tough and wanted to get back to a more familiar and sheltered en-vironment. Unfortunately there is not really such a simple means of escaping from the world, however distant it may seem and however attractive a parochial way of life may be in the United States. Americans themselves who had to compete with this ignorance were well aware of it, and I am reminded of the story of the famous American Commander-in-Chief who, when descended upon by a group of Senators, would sit them down in front of a map and begin by explaining: 'That is the land, and the blue is the sea!'

The second point is that Americans have always shown a desire to duck and have never been slow to find every excuse to do so, particularly if they can satisfy themselves that the main reason is moral. After all, three Presidents have been happily elected or re-elected on a no-war ticket. President Wilson in 1916 and President Roosevelt in 1940 were both able to claim as their chief vote-catching slogan: 'I kept you out of the war.' It was President Johnson's main platform in 1964, when he overwhelmingly defeated Senator Goldwater, and yet all these Presidents had to go into a war unprepared, and knew that they would have to go into a war, to defend America's vital interests.

It is that which gives me the right to speak. The initial brunt of World Wars I and II was taken by Britain and France while the United States slept (except to make money). Both these wars cost my own country particularly dear. My father's generation in World War I was decimated and my own genera-tion in World War II suffered casualties incomparably greater than those suffered by the same generation in the United States. Next time there is not going to be a Europe to take the brunt and, if the United States are still asleep, they may suffer a rude awakening which will make Pearl Harbour look like a Sunday picnic. Worse still, they may find themselves in a situation where the mere threat will be enough to crumble their will to resist.

If, under the umbrella of deterrence and *détente* protracted wars and political violence continue or even increase, as seems likely, then the West must come to terms with them. This requires a revision of attitude. Gone are the days when the logical and rational minds in Western capitals could work out (and enforce) reasonable compromise solutions to conflict which would restore peace. The men of violence have learnt that they do not have to accept compromise solutions even when the concessions are higher than they have earned. All they have to do is take the concessions and increase the violence. In these circumstances a bad agreement is worse than no agreement at all. The only answer, where solutions or settlements (as in Vietnam or the Middle East and elsewhere) prove intractable and the prospect of a lasting peace seems hopeless, is to refuse concessions and to establish a state of 'stable war',[1] in which neither side can achieve victory by force or upset the *de facto* situation with impunity. Out of that deadlock a just solution may emerge. This, in turn, requires that the United States should seek to maintain a balance of power at all levels, from nuclear downwards, and in all areas of potential conflict. Unfortunately no one has yet invented an alternative to a balance of power except an imbalance of power. It is that present imbalance, resulting mainly from the Vietnam war and its effect on American will and stamina, which could lead to the dangerous situation put forward at the end of this book.

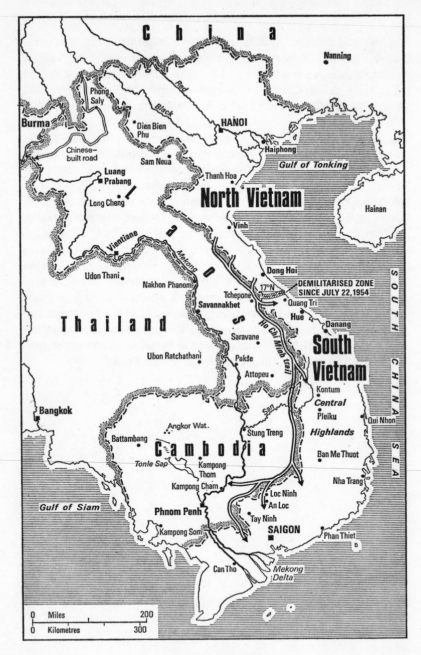

Map 1. Indochina

CHAPTER I

WHOSE WAR?

On Sunday, 5 January, 1969, after Mr. Richard Nixon had been elected but before his inauguration as President, I travelled up to London to see Mr. Lee Kuan Yew, the Prime Minister of Singapore, at his request. We had known each other for many years and I regard him as the most realistic statesman in South East Asia. When I entered his room in the Hyde Park Hotel he said at once as he greeted me: 'They've lost, haven't they?'

He did not base his statement on the current situation in Vietnam, in Paris or in the United States, but relied on the view that many people held at that time with regard to President Nixon. For some years the war in Vietnam had been acclaimed as Johnson's war and President Johnson himself had been unseated by it. How therefore could President Nixon now conceivably stay with it and turn it into Nixon's war? During the course of the 1968 Presidential election Mr. Nixon had been in the enviable position of being able to advocate an end to the war through a negotiated settlement, while rejecting the concept of imposing a coalition or a solution by force on Saigon, without having to say how he would go about it. Now he was about to inherit the mess. It was not surprising that there were many who thought that he might take the easy way out by maintaining that it was Kennedy's and Johnson's war, that the Democrats had lost it and that he was getting out.

I must admit that over the previous six months I had had very serious doubts myself whether the situation could be saved, not because of what needed to be done in South Vietnam itself during the new Administration—that I had already discussed with Dr. Henry Kissinger when he was still foreign affairs adviser to Governor Nelson Rockefeller—but because the American will to do it seemed to be completely lacking. I had been in the United States during the previous summer at the time of Senator Robert Kennedy's assassination and had witnessed the shock which this had delivered to the system.

Just after it I had, in fact, addressed the Council on Foreign Relations in New York on the theme that, while the war in Vietnam might still be won, I regarded it as lost because I did not see that the United States had either the will or the competence to restore the situation. With the events in Chicago, which followed at the Democratic Convention, and the absurd line subsequently taken by Vice-President Humphrey during his election campaign that having lost the war he could win peace, this view was reinforced. Then came the halting of the bombing by President Johnson on 1 November, a few days before the election, in a last-ditch attempt to swing the election in favour of Mr. Humphrey. This politically cynical act did not exactly restore my faith. However, Mr. Nixon was elected and this, coupled with President Thieu's determined refusal to be stampeded by President Johnson in his last days in office into accepting a peace at any price settlement, at least temporarily stopped the rot. While, therefore, I was half inclined to agree with Mr. Lee Kuan Yew that 'They have lost, haven't they?', I hedged and said that we ought to wait and see how President Nixon handled it after he was inaugurated. I had no doubt at all that, like everyone else, he wanted to end the war but not at any price. He had always been firm on one point—that no form of government, including a coalition, would be imposed on the South Vietnamese by force and that they must be given a chance to determine their own future.

If President Nixon tried to achieve that objective during his term of office, would that really make it Nixon's war instead of Johnson's war? Going back, was it ever Johnson's or Kennedy's war, or, for that matter, an American war? Two questions which have to be answered are: Whose war was it? And what did winning the war mean in terms of both North and South Vietnam?

There are three main factors in Vietnamese history which have had an influence on the present war and the struggle for power in Indochina: the heritage and proximity of China, which have been the dominating political influences for over 2,000 years; the dynastic rebellions in Vietnam which have always divided and ravaged the country; and *Nam Tien* or the advance southwards from the original cradle of the Vietnamese, as a people and a country, in the Red River basin of the present North Vietnam.

The Vietnamese people were originally a 'barbarian' race on the southern borders of the Chinese Empire and, for 1,000 years from 111 B.C. to A.D. 938, their territory was directly administered as a province of China. To the Chinese the Vietnamese owed their language, literature, culture, religions, agricultural system and the administrative structure of their government. For the following 900 years, until the coming of the French in the nineteenth century, the ruling dynasties of Vietnam acknowledged Chinese suzerainty. China was constantly intervening, generally by invitation, in Vietnam's dynastic squabbles but never succeeded, except for a short period in the Ming Dynasty, in re-imposing direct Chinese rule. Even Kublai Khan failed. French, British, Americans or even Russians may appear upon the scene for a brief period, but China must inevitably remain the dominant influence, historically and geographically, on the Vietnamese scene.

The Vietnam which became independent in A.D. 938 was roughly equivalent to the present North Vietnam with its capital where Hanoi now stands. For the next 700 years the territory of Vietnam under the first Le, the Ly, the Tran, the Ho and the second Le dynasties, except for brief intervals under a strong emperor, was racked by invasion, rebellion and turbulence. The succession was never secure and at times emperor followed emperor each to be murdered after a few months. Nevertheless the Chinese to the north were held at bay either by diplomacy or battle, while Vietnam steadily expanded southwards at the expense of the Cham Empire (based on the present central Vietnam or Annam). At the beginning of the seventeenth century, during the latter part of the second Le dynasty, the Nguyen family in the South in opposition to the powerful Trinh family in the North divided Vietnam into two separate parts, with the dividing line near Dong Hoi just north of the 17th Parallel (the present DMZ). These two parts became rival states having neither diplomatic relations nor trade with each other. There followed a long period of relative peace until the Tay Son rebellion in 1771 under the three Ho brothers.[2] This rebellion, which resulted in the capture of Qui

3

Nhon in 1773, encouraged the Trinhs to invade the South, but the usurping Ho brothers having occupied the whole of the South (Cochin-China), invaded the North and eliminated the Trinh family. The brothers divided the whole of Vietnam between them, nominally as the protectors of the Le emperor.

But Nguyen Phuoc Anh, the rightful Nguyen heir in the South, in spite of having to flee to the off-shore islands and subsequently Siam, fought back. He landed at Ha Tien in the extreme south in 1787 and recaptured Saigon in 1788. He pressed slowly but steadily northward, capturing Hue in 1801 and the whole of Vietnam in 1802, and proclaimed himself Emperor under the title of Gia Long while continuing to recognize Chinese suzerainty. He had unified what are now the present territories of Vietnam for the first and only time. Nevertheless, having established his court at Hue, he divided the country administratively into the three regions of Tonkin, Annam and Cochin-China. Under his incompetent and decadent successors, however, all this disintegrated so that the country fell an easy prey to, and was absorbed into, the French colonial empire. China's suzerainty was formally ended by the Treaty of Tientsin in 1885. The French maintained the three administrative regions, with Cochin-China as a colony and with Tonkin and Annam as protectorates under the nominal sovereignty of the Nguyen Emperor. When French rule ended in 1954 Vietnam was again left divided, almost exactly at the same point as in the seventeenth and eighteenth centuries.

The third influential factor was the *Nam Tien* or advance southwards. From the dawn of time Vietnam had always been a passageway for people moving south, some of whom have stayed or been left behind, such as the Montagnard tribes. For example, the late Mr. Richard Noone, a well-known anthropologist in South East Asia, found that one Malayan aboriginal tribe, which passed through Vietnam several thousand years ago, was closely akin in culture and language to one of the Montagnard tribes and that they could still speak to each other. This procession has been continual and the Vietnamese have been the last in the chain moving south in search of additional rice land. That movement is still going on—no one moves north.

4

Over 900 years ago the Cham king first ceded territory in Quang Tri to the Vietnamese who, by the beginning of the fourteenth century, had reached Hue. It was a gradual advance, the present provinces of Quang Nam and Quang Ngai being gained a hundred years later. Not until 1611 did the Vietnamese reach Phu Yen. The Cham Empire (Champa) finally ceased to exist as a separate state in 1693 when its territories were annexed as part of Cochin-China by the Nguyen dynasty of South Vietnam. All the time, however, settlers were migrating southwards well ahead of their government and frequently to avoid it. (Sociologists might note that they were not held back by devotion to their ancestral lands.) By the beginning of the eighteenth century the present southern provinces of South Vietnam had been annexed from the decaying Khmer (Cambodian) Empire to give the South Vietnamese the Mekong Delta which was to become one of the richest rice-growing areas in the world. It is this wealth that the hardy Tonkinese so greedily covet from their softer Cochin-Chinese brothers in a continuing advance southwards.

The present war has, therefore, been perfectly comprehensible in its historical context within Indochina, but in the last thirty years it was further complicated by the addition of the ideological doctrine of communism, thereby bringing the expressed expansionary aims of that doctrine into a direct clash with the democratic but defensive policies of the Western world.

The first Indochina war from 1946 to 1954 between the Vietminh and the declining French Empire established the contestants and the issues for the second Indochina war beginning in 1959. The basic local issue was, and still is, the succession to French power in Indochina. But the war was more than that. If it had been no more than a straight power struggle between warring nationalist factions then it would have been a continuing repetition of Vietnamese history, but, with the foundation of the Indochinese Communist Party under Ho Chi Minh, its seizure of power in the North immediately after World War II and the elimination of its nationalist rivals, the issue of the succession became more fundamental to the people of Indochina. It was not just a question of driving out the French and

5

establishing independent Vietnamese rule again with a dynastic or even a republican form of government, because the communist party was seeking, in addition to the succession to power, the complete transformation politically, socially and culturally of the whole society. It was not a rebellion or civil war as in the past, but a revolution in Marxist-Leninist terms which would ensure that the Indochinese Communist Party secured the succession and then remained in unchallengeable power indefinitely. It was also in the context of the cold war of some importance internationally, particularly after the victory of Mao Tse Tung in China. Without China as the 'great rear base' and without trucks, supplies and, above all, artillery from China at Dien Bien Phu, the Vietminh would not have been successful. It was the victory of the Chinese Communist Party which made the victory of the Indochina Communist Party possible. China was playing both its traditional role of intervention to secure a friendly and grateful government on its southern flank and its new ideological role of communist expansion and world revolution.

This naturally created its counter-force. The military core of this was initially the French expeditionary force, but politically the French were supported by large groupings of nationalist Vietnamese, Cambodians and Laotians who, while they did not want the French, desired still less the dictatorship of a (mainly Vietnamese) communist party. The French were therefore able to build up considerable local forces and, at the same time, gained international Western support, including military and financial assistance from the United States as a result of the Korean war. After Greece and Korea the West was in no mood to tolerate communist aggression or the imposition of communist dictatorships by force. The cornerstone of American and Western defence policy at this time was the 1947 Truman doctrine: 'It must be the policy of the United States to support free peoples who are resisting attempted subjugation by armed minorities or by outside pressures.'

The death of Stalin, the East German uprising in 1953 (put down by Russian tanks) and the failure in 1954 of the Berlin Conference to settle the Berlin question inclined the new leaders in Russia to seek a settlement in the Far East both in

Korea and Indochina. Pressure was brought to bear on the Vietminh and this compelled General Vo Nguyen Giap, as the Geneva Conference opened, to seek and gain a quick military victory at Dien Bien Phu, at an enormous cost in lives, in order to break the French will to continue fighting and to obtain the best possible terms. As a result of the Geneva Agreements[3] in 1954, the Vietminh were required to evacuate Laos and Cambodia, which were established as independent sovereign states. Vietnam once again was temporarily divided at the 17th Parallel. At least these Agreements did for a time separate the parties and their armed forces, but they did not provide a permanent solution and certainly did not recognize the Vietminh claim to hegemony in Indochina as the successors to the French.

This prompted the first myth to arise from the Geneva Agreements — that the Vietminh were disappointed with the result and had been robbed of complete victory. It was, however, the Vietminh who first put forward the idea of partition. Both they and the Malenkov Government in Russia were probably influenced by the practical certainty of being able to establish a new communist state in North Vietnam by accepting an immediate settlement and thereby eliminating the risks of the French continuing the war and of possible direct American intervention. The myth was finally exploded by the Khrushchev Memoirs. When the French proposed that the division of Vietnam should be at the 17th Parallel, Khrushchev wrote: 'I will confess that when we were informed of this news from Geneva, we gasped with surprise and pleasure. We had not expected anything like this. The 17th Parallel was the absolute maximum we would have claimed ourselves.' What the Russians, the Chinese (at that time still aligned with Russia) and the Vietminh appreciated was that their extensive gain of territory in North Vietnam could be consolidated as an irrevocably communist state and used as a base for a further advance later. This is a constant communist stratagem — grab a bit, gain recognition of it as a *fait accompli*, then prepare to grab the next bit.

The second myth which arose out of the Geneva Agreements was the election issue for the re-unification of Vietnam. The

7

final Declaration[4] provided that there should be consultations between the two parties so that a free election could be held in 1956, throughout Vietnam, to decide both on unification and the future government of the country. The failure to hold such an election is constantly cited as a valid excuse for the Vietcong uprising within the South and the invasion of the South by the North. The provision was so worded that the votes of the two parts were to be combined, which meant that the votes of the numerically superior North (by about two million people) would outweigh those of the South. It was not to be a separate vote in each territory whereby, within the South, a majority voting against unification would have prevailed. Moreover, the Declaration was not an agreement and was not signed by any of the members of the Conference. When, therefore, the time came for consultations on the election, the Government of South Vietnam, supported by the United States, refused to hold such an election on the perfectly legitimate grounds that the voting in the North could not be free, as required by the Declaration, and that its numerically superior vote would give the South no say whatsoever in its own future, even if everyone voted against unification.

If that procedure was to be applied to a divided Vietnam in 1956, then why not to East and West Germany, where a free West German vote would always have outweighed a solid communist East German vote? That argument silenced Russia which, while initially supporting the North Vietnamese demand for such an election, did not press it. Russia could not have accepted the challenge under any circumstances of a similar vote either on a divided Germany or a divided Korea.

The election myth was given further prominence by the frequent misquoting of President Eisenhower to the effect that in any free election after 1954 Ho Chi Minh would have won 80 per cent of the votes in both North and South Vietnam. In fact, what Eisenhower said was that 'had elections been held as of the time of the fighting, possibly 80 per cent of the population would have voted for the Communist Ho Chi Minh as their leader rather than Chief of State Bao Dai'.[5] But that was neither the time nor the choice. In the event what happened after 1954 was that the authorities in both North and South took steps to establish themselves as separate governments and sovereign states and, in terms of international law, both succeeded—rather better in the South where there was at least a referendum on this issue. In 1955, in that referendum, the South voted overwhelmingly to establish a separate republic of South Vietnam by a 99 per cent vote. This may have been manipulated but not by more than 10 per cent. President Diem was not at that time firmly in the saddle (it was this vote which put him in as President). The North was given no similar opportunity to vote on its future or its government. The Lao Dong Party was in full control and no ballot box nor revolt, such as was carried out in 1956 by the peasants of Thanh Hoa and Nghe An provinces, was going to throw it out. Even Russia at that time was prepared to recognize South Vietnam and to agree to the membership of both South and North in the United Nations, but the package deal fell through over the same recognition for the two Germanys. In any case neither North Vietnam nor the Communist Powers were interested in the ballot box as a means of determining the future of South Vietnam, or for that matter any other country. (It had failed them dismally, in spite of Russian military occupation, in Hungary and Czechoslovakia after World War II.) On the contrary they have always been scared of the ballot box and, over the succeeding twenty years in South Vietnam, with some justification. The paramount point which comes through the whole of the Vietnam war, including the period after the ceasefire, is that the North Vietnamese and the Vietcong never had any hope of winning the South politically through elections. It could only be taken by violence and force, even if that meant a massive military invasion after the techniques of revolutionary war had failed.

In every election held in South Vietnam, for whatever purpose and irrespective of the parties and candidates, the South Vietnamese were voting to remain separate and independent. In this respect two important elections were those for the Constituent Assembly in 1966 and subsequently for the Presidency in 1967.

It will be remembered that South Vietnam was close to

collapse after the fall of President Diem at the end of 1963 and the following disastrous year of 1964 under General Khanh. American troops had landed in March, 1965, and battles were raging in 1966 throughout the country with large populated areas under Vietcong control. Nevertheless, when a Constituent Assembly was elected to draw up a new constitution for the South—in other words for a separate independent government and country—out of an estimated population of 17 millions, of whom about 7 millions were of voting age (18), the registered number of voters was 5,288,572. The number of votes cast was 4,274,872—that is 80·8 per cent of the registered voters and between 55 and 60 per cent of all those eligible. The turnout and the percentages were about normal for most western countries but, with the disruption of war and with the Vietcong instructing voters to boycott the election and using terror to intimidate them, the turnout was remarkably high and demonstrated the outstanding feature of all the elections—the determination of the South Vietnamese people not to be deterred, whatever the threat, from having a say in their own future.

This Constituent Assembly drew up the new constitution and passed the electoral laws for subsequent elections to the Presidency, the Senate and the Lower House. It also laid down that no known communists should be allowed to stand. On that point the ruling military junta, nominally under the Prime Ministership of Air Vice-Marshal Nguyen Cao Ky, had the support of the An Quang (Buddhist) party which, after having played a prominent part in the overthrow of President Diem, was regarded as the main opposition party.

In the elections which followed the most interesting was that for the Presidency. There were eleven candidates with their respective running mates. The number of registered voters was by this time 5,853,251 of whom 4,735,404 voted. The result was that, out of the eleven candidates, the Thieu and Ky ticket got 34·8 per cent. I cannot believe that, in a similar vote in either the United Kingdom or the United States with eleven candidates, including several from each of the two major parties, any individual would get such a high percentage. Of the remaining tickets an estimated 35 per cent would have backed Thieu in a run-off. For example, the Huong ticket which gained 10 per cent of the votes must be regarded as basically pro-Thieu because Tran Van Huong himself became Thieu's first Prime Minister and, in 1971, his running mate and Vice-President. I have excluded from this 35 per cent the Buddhist vote for the ticket led by Pham Khac Suu (10·8 per cent) because, at that time, the Buddhists were not only opposed to Thieu and Ky but might have been regarded as neutral in the war effort. Their main support was in the northern provinces round Hue; and the Vietcong massacre in Hue, which completely altered the Buddhist stand, did not occur until the Tet offensive in 1968. But the vote which attracted the most international and public attention was the 17·2 per cent gained by the Dzu and Chieu ticket, which had canvassed on a peace platform and came second. Truong Dinh Dzu himself, being a lawyer of questionable repute in Saigon, was of little account but probably attracted any Vietcong supporters who were inclined to vote. What escaped comment was that his running mate Tran Van Chieu was a member of the Cao Dai religious sect whose Papal seat is established in Tay Ninh and whose strength lay in that and other nearby provinces north of Saigon. It was in this Cao Dai area that the ticket gained its greatest success, which suggests that the vote was for Chieu rather than Dzu. (After the Vietcong attack on Tay Ninh at the time of the ceasefire, which at one point threatened the Cao Dai temple, had been denounced by the Cao Dai Pope, that vote would now go solidly to President Thieu—see Chapter VIII.)

The next elections of any consequence were those three or four years later for the Senate, in 1970, and for the Lower House and the re-election of Thieu as President in 1971. The Senate has an unusual election system for its 60 members in that they stand country wide in slates of 10 members each. At the first election in September, 1967, there had been 48 such slates—that is 480 candidates. The leading six of the slates in the votes cast throughout the country, therefore, provided the senators. The government-backed slate had come in third. The first slate was led by a former Diem general and the fifth by Thieu's subsequent Foreign Minister Tram Van Lam (later in 1973 Chairman of the Senate). When it came to the second

Senate elections in 1970 half the Senators retired and there were three new slates of ten members each to be elected. The winning slate was the Buddhist opposition slate led by Vu Van Mau (one time Foreign Minister to Diem) which gained 40,000 votes more than the government-backed second slate. The fourth, but unsuccessful, slate was also government-backed and gained just under 800,000 votes. A general analysis of the total voting for all slates showed that government supporters (who only got 10 out of the 30 seats) gained about 50 per cent of the votes cast, independents 25 per cent and the opposition 25 per cent, which in any parliamentary democracy would be regarded as a fair measure of support.

In talking here of opposition it is necessary to be more precise. It means opposition to the government on many of its policies and, naturally, a desire to be in office. It does not necessarily mean opposition to the war or to Thieu's conduct of it. The nearest analogy, though not exact, was Churchill's position on the war issue in the 1940s in the House of Commons (for which, as compared with South Vietnam, no general election was held until the end of the war with Germany). I have spoken to many members of this so-called opposition in Vietnam who, on the fundamental issue of the war—a separate independent South Vietnamese state—have made such remarks as: 'I would prefer President Thieu, even if he became a dictator, to a coalition government.' And in 1973 the same opposition Senator told me that, as far as he was concerned, on that issue Thieu could have the Presidency for life.

An equally revealing election was that on 29 August, 1971, for the Lower House. There were 1,239 candidates for 159 seats in a country which some write off as a dictatorship. In one Saigon constituency alone, for the election of 5 seats, there were 80 candidates. This meant that each voter had to be given sheets of forms and symbols from which he had to select and mark the five for whom he was voting. The queues were long but by this time nearly all Vietnamese, at every level of elections, had come to take their voting duty very seriously. The turnout was 5,567,446 out of just over 7 million registered voters in a rising population of between 18 and 19 millions of whom, with at least a 3 per cent annual increase, well over 50 per cent were under 18. The general estimate of the result was that government supporters gained 80–90 seats, the opposition 55–60 with 10–15 independents. The honesty of this election was never questioned but received little coverage.

Finally, there was the most controversial election of them all—the re-election of President Thieu as President in October, 1971. It had been decided, quite rightly, that there could no longer be a free-for-all as on the previous occasion with a multiplicity of candidates. It might perhaps have been better if the French run-off system had been adopted. Instead the GVN, with the approval of the Lower House and the Senate, decided that candidates must be in a position to show that they had a reasonable measure of public support to justify their nomination. It was therefore required that any candidate should be sponsored by a certain number either of members of the House and Senate or members of the elected Provincial Councils. The first issue of importance was whether President Thieu would again accept Air Vice-Marshal Ky as his running mate. This had been necessary in 1967 to prevent a split in the armed forces, but that was no longer a consideration. Thieu selected the much respected Huong, who had been his first Prime Minister in 1967, and Ky therefore became a rival candidate. As an exiled Northerner Ky never had a chance and his whole campaign was designed, not to gain sufficient support for nomination which he could have mustered, nor to campaign seriously for the Presidency, but to embarrass and compel Thieu into giving him a suitable appointment. In this he failed but was allowed to retain his official house, car and salary, and subsequently became a successful farmer.

The only serious rival candidate was the former Diem General, Duong Van Minh, better known as 'Big Minh'. His first claim to fame was when, as a Colonel immediately after President Diem came to power, he commanded the forces which threw out and annihilated the Binh Xuyen bandits who in 1954 ran a protection racket in Saigon controlling the gambling and the brothels. In 1963 he had led the group of ARVN Generals who carried out the coup against President Diem and then murdered him. During his subsequent period in power he had shown himself to be easy-going, indecisive and incompetent. He had no positive policies whatsoever for running the country, which soon began to fall apart. However, within three months he was overthrown in a second coup by General Khanh but, because he was a popular figure with some attraction for foreign observers and press correspondents, was retained by General Khanh as nominal Head of State during 1964. In 1965, when the junta of younger military generals took over, he retired for a period to Bangkok and did not return to contest the 1967 Presidential election. Many have mistakenly attributed his popular appeal to the overthrow of Diem, whereas in fact he carries the blame for the murder of Diem for which many in the country have not forgiven him. Moreover, there has never been any accounting for the jewels and currency which were in Diem's possession at the time of his murder. The officer who handed Diem's briefcase over has not been seen again. Finally, Vietnamese do not readily give political support to someone who has had his chance and who, after only three months in power, is then caught napping in bed by a rival. Nevertheless, he had some following and was a person round whom some, but not all, of the opposition to Thieu might have rallied. This made him the only possible alternative candidate, but the question was whether he would stand.

I happened to be in Saigon for the first three months of 1971 and reached the conclusion, in which I was not alone, that Thieu had such overwhelming support that 'Big Minh' would be unlikely to get 20 per cent of the vote. This would have finished him as a political figure. Accordingly, on 1 April, 1971, over six months before the election, I wrote to Dr. Henry Kissinger and on this point said:

'On the political front all the present indications are that Thieu has really got it made for 4 October. It is becoming almost impossible to see an opponent of any stature giving him a close race. There is even a fear that he could obtain such an overwhelming majority that the sceptics in the United States would not believe it. I can almost foresee someone like Big Minh, realising that he has no hope, provoking such an American reaction by getting up in August and saying that, because the elections are bound to be dirty, he does not intend to stand.'

That is exactly what happened.

On 4 October, 1971, in spite of there being no opposition candidate, 6,327,631 South Vietnamese went to the polls, about 760,000 more than for the Lower House elections a few weeks before. There were of course no vast queues because there was only one ballot paper, but at least in Saigon where I watched it there was a steady stream throughout the day. This turnout was 87·9 per cent of the registered voters. There was every opportunity to show opposition either by staying away or by spoiling the ballot paper, and this was done either by defacing it or throwing it in the waste paper basket provided. Out of the total, 356,000 voters did just that, but nearly 6 million cast valid votes for their President.

I would be the last to suggest that all the election figures quoted[6] are dead accurate, or that they were not made to look a bit better than was the case in some provinces, but I am convinced that in all elections since 1966 the figures have been within five per cent and that anyone who brushes elections in South Vietnam aside as being corrupt and worthless is only doing it because the results do not suit his political view. Those like myself,[7] who watched the school teachers and respectable matrons of Saigon counting the ballot papers in the 1971 Presidential election and holding them up, whether correct or defaced, for all to see, could only regard the arrangements and their behaviour as exemplary. I made a note through samples of the counting as to the number defaced in various batches of 50 or 100 and this corresponded very closely with the final overall total throughout the country.

But it is not my point, nor my task, to validate the results of South Vietnamese elections. I have used them as a statistic to show not that the Vietnamese were voting for this person or that person at any particular election, but that they were consistently voting for those who were prepared to lead them in upholding a separate independent South Vietnamese state. It has of course been one of the fundamental errors on the American scene, and for the sake of its simplicity probably always will be, to identify the leader with the state and the people. How often has the war been expressed as Diem's war, or Ky's war, or Thieu's war? How often has some protester or politician put the question: 'Why should we send American boys to fight for Thieu?' I must admit that when such a question is put to me I am rendered almost speechless by its sheer stupidity. It suggests that the whole American effort in World War II was intended solely to keep Stalin and Churchill in power. In any case, why Thieu, when in little more than ten years there have been President Diem, 'Big Minh', General Khanh, Prime Minister Huong, Prime Minister Quat and Air Vice-Marshal Ky before Thieu ever became President? This convinces me that if it was not Thieu the South Vietnamese people would still be fighting led by someone else. But why not Thieu? He is unquestionably the best leader[8] the South Vietnamese have had and has carried them through great crises which would have felled lesser contemporary figures on the world stage today.

On many visits to South Vietnamese units and villages this point has always been brought home to me but never more so than when I visited a hamlet on the northern bank of the Thu Thua canal, in Long An province, just after the ceasefire in 1973. This canal links the two rivers which flow down on either side of the Parrot's Beak close to the Cambodian border and is the first physical obstacle in that area to North Vietnamese invading forces. The houses are sited along the banks of the canal but the rice fields extend into the Plain of Reeds towards the border only fifteen miles away. It was one of the hundreds of hamlets which the North Vietnamese had tried to grab in the nights following the ceasefire. It was defended by the volunteer part-time unpaid members of the People's Self Defence Force (similar to the Home Guard) supported by a full-time paid Popular Force platoon composed of young men from the village. The nearest reinforcement was a Regional Force company further along the canal under the control of the district headquarters, again composed of young men from the province. There were no regular army troops. This was by no means the first time the area had been attacked, but without any fuss the enemy was engaged and, although casualties were suffered and houses were burnt down, the attack was driven off. The

16

villagers were not elated by their victory and in the face of their hamlet chief, who had been wounded in the hand by an AK47 bullet, you could see a quiet determination that if it happened again, as it would, they would do it again. Their families were there, their land was there, their houses were expendable but repairable. Some of them would die, others would take their place. They would keep their enemy out.

In the light of all the evidence, which is so readily available about the state of agriculture in communist countries, I have never understood why so many people can think that the people of South Vietnam, who so obviously enjoy free enterprise and whose peasants own the land they cultivate, should welcome or support those who are intent on collectivization. The war has always been, and still is being, fought in the South by the people both, as in past Vietnamese history, against a northern invader, and, in the present, to preserve their own way of life against an alien ideology and form of government. That this would be the case was always understood by Lenin, as shown in his article on partisan warfare originally published in 1906. He referred to Kautsky's prediction in 1902 that the coming revolution would not be so much a struggle of the people against the government, as a struggle of one part of the people against the other, and added: 'It is natural and unavoidable that . . . the uprising cannot assume the traditional form of a single blow limited to a very short time and a very small area. It is natural and unavoidable that the uprising assumes the higher and more complicated form of a protracted civil war enmeshing the entire country—that is the form of armed struggle by one part of the people against the other.' In exactly that way the great majority of the people of the South have fought first against the Vietcong and then against the North Vietnamese Army.

It is their war and, what is more, they know what it is about,[9] as did Lenin when he said: 'When we Bolsheviks established a dictatorship of the proletariat, the workers became more hungry, and their standard of living went down; the victory of the workers is impossible without sacrifices, without a temporary worsening of the situation.' While it is interesting to note than he referred to 'their' standard of living, not his or our, the point that 'temporary' lasted for a long time in both Russia and North Vietnam, and that most communist countries still require to be partly fed by the free enterprise West, has not been lost on the agricultural peasant community of South Vietnam.

CHAPTER II

THE COMPREHENSIBILITY GAP

The stake of the South Vietnamese people in staying separate and independent is best shown by the intent of the Politburo in Hanoi. What would happen if North Vietnam took over? In the summer of 1972 I was invited by the *New York Times Magazine* to answer that exact question in the following cable:

> *New York Times Magazine* would very much like you to write a 2,500-word scenario on what will happen when North Vietnam takes over South Vietnam to include what you see as possible slaughter, but also to go beyond that to describe the kind of government that would be set up, the action that government might take internally, domestically and internationally; who would be the leaders of that government and how would they be chosen? What would happen to Buddhists, Catholics and other non-communist groups, etc.? This would be used as companion piece for a more benign view of the probable outcome of the North's takeover.

Accordingly in August, 1972, I sent them the following article entitled 'There would have been a bloodbath':

> The question as to what would have happened if the North Vietnamese invasion had been successful and if the North had taken over the South is fast becoming hypothetical. With the Vietcong reduced to a negligible internal threat in a few traditional base areas, with the North Vietnamese Army's massive invasion already blunted and with pacification and Vietnamisation only dented by it, the South Vietnamese are once again showing their extraordinary resilience and their capacity to survive as a separate independent state.
>
> That independence would have been the first casualty of defeat. However much lip service may have been paid, for external propaganda purposes, to the National Liberation Front and the Provisional Revolutionary Government, the

Politburo in Hanoi has throughout been determined on the re-unification of Vietnam. This has come through in every speech and article by its members. As Prime Minister Pham Van Dong said at the 3rd Party Congress in 1960: "Behind many contrasting 'fronts', the Party has never swerved from the purpose of bringing the Vietnamese people under its revolutionary regime." He added that these fronts had worked "for the single-minded goal of re-unification under socialism." The policy is even embodied in the North's constitution, Article 7, which reads: "The State strictly prohibits and punishes all acts of treason, opposition to the peoples' democratic system, or opposition to the re-unification of the fatherland."

After all, if re-unification was not the North's primary policy, why else would its leaders have so tragically sent, over the last ten years, nearly a million of their youth to death or wounds in the South and destroyed a whole generation? Why, when the Vietcong were doing so well after the fall of President Diem, did Hanoi insert regular North Vietnamese Army units in 1964 other than to secure the fruits of victory? Again, why in 1968 did General Vo Nguyen Giap put Vietcong units into the forefront of the Tet offensive to be almost wiped out?* The recent invasion has been conducted almost entirely by the NVA. All the so-called Vietcong units, which were marginally involved inside South Vietnam, contained more than 50 per cent fillers from the NVA. Does anyone really suppose that, if the invasion had succeeded, an independent state under the NLF would have been established? Re-unification would have been the certain result whatever the wishes of the South Vietnamese people.

What sort of government would then have been imposed? Certainly the present Politburo in Hanoi, as the leaders of the Indochina Communist Party and the Vietnam Workers' Party, would have been in full control and would have brought "the Vietnamese people under its revolutionary regime". But would the government have been a coalition? In our sense no, because it would not have contained any members of the present GVN nor even of the many other

* See p. 84 below.

nationalist parties now operating within South Vietnam. But it might have been called a coalition because it would have contained members of the "Democratic Party" and the "Socialist Party" (and any other shells you like to mention). These parties are a distinction without a difference. The statutes of the former describe its purpose as "representing the bourgeoisie and helping it to participate in the struggle for creation of a peaceful *unified* powerful and prosperous Vietnam in accordance with the policies of the working class and the Workers' Party", while the Socialist Party represents "intellectuals in close association and tight unity with the Workers' Party". One member of the last is Nguyen Huu Tho, the present Chairman of the National Liberation Front.

There would have been established in the South, below the Politburo, a hierarchy of peoples' committees and councils composed of local men and headed perhaps by Nguyen Huu Tho, with each echelon technically electing the next higher but receiving its instructions downwards from it, i.e. "democratic centralism". The point here is that the Politburo accepts the Stalin view (as reiterated in 1969 in *Nhan Dan*, the Hanoi daily newspaper) that "the party is an instrument of proletarian dictatorship; the party is a one-minded bloc that does not admit factional organisations within its ranks ..."

The legislature would have been a National Assembly whose powers would have been exercised by a standing committee, of which the Chairman in the North is Truong Chinh, the number two ranking member of the Politburo. The full Assembly in the North only meets twice a year and was in fact in session between 1967 and 1970 for only four days. This compares somewhat unfavourably with the present legislature in the South which is in session for about six months each year and is exceedingly critical of the Government. Candidates for the National Assembly "must have struggled for unification and be in absolute accord with socialism". They are proportionate in the North to the classes in the community such as the army, workers, farmers, intellectuals and so on. The actual candidates are selected by the "Fatherland front" in the name of the party and are presented to the people in lists of about a dozen and those voting may strike out any two names. This again compares somewhat unfavourably with the Lower House in South Vietnam where last year there were 1,239 candidates for 159 seats. In one Saigon constituency alone there were 80 candidates for 5 seats.*

The second casualty, therefore, of a North Vietnamese take-over would have been the budding democracy of South Vietnam. But, you will say, is not President Thieu himself also a dictator? On this point it is worth quoting the view of his opposition. A leading opposition Senator of the An Quang Buddhists said to me only three months ago, in front of five reporters, that he "preferred President Thieu, even if he *became* a dictator, to a coalition government".* Ex-Foreign Minister, Dr. Tran Van Do, a respected elder statesman who holds no candle for President Thieu, was recently quoted in U.S. News and World Report as saying: "There is certainly much corruption and incompetence in our society but it is open for all to see. We have fought a war and tried to build a democracy at the same time. Sometimes I think I would have preferred a dictatorship during the fighting. It would have been more effective; it is what the other side has. But we have opened everything, all our faults, for everybody to see; we have paid a very great price for democracy."

Under a communist dictatorship you can forget all the freedoms. There is of course no need for censorship because all the media are a government monopoly. After a suitable interval some tame foreign journalists might have been allowed in but the first departures from South Vietnam for sure would have been every one of the 392 accredited foreign journalists, not many of whom are tame to either side. Even a poor little "pop" group in the North recently received savage sentences, ranging from 15 years to 18 months, for "disseminating depraved imperialist culture and counter-revolutionary propaganda". As Truong Chinh [Number two ranking member of the Politburo] has stated, "one can create a new socialist Vietnamese music". But obviously you cannot do your thing!

* See Chapter I, p. 12.

With regard to religions such as Buddhism and Catholicism, they would have been allowed to continue meeting as religious groups and to hold services, but under committees of management approved by the party and dedicated to requiring their members to carry out the party line. Tran Quoc Hoan, Minister of Security in March of this year, in a massive article on struggling against counter-revolution, made some remarks about Catholicism: "Generally speaking any person or organisation that hates the revolution . . . or opposes the struggle for peace and national unification must be considered counter-revolutionary. . . . The most notable of these are reactionaries who take advantage of Catholicism." It must not be forgotten, moreover, that the great majority of refugees from North Vietnam in 1954, numbering over 800,000, were Catholics whose village settlements in South Vietnam subsequently became bastions of self-defence against the Vietcong. Hundreds of thousands of Catholics and of the Hoa Hao and Cao Dai Sects would, because of their resolute resistance, have been placed on the "blood-debt" list and destined at worst for execution or labour camps and at best for thought reform.

In the same article Tran Quoc Hoan also referred to "the counter-revolutionary riots in Hungary in 1956 and the 'peaceful evolution' plot in Czechoslovakia in 1968" as "profound lessons", which suggests that, in foreign policy, the unified state would have inclined towards Russia rather than China. I think it probable, however, that the new state would have attempted to steer a middle course as between Russia and China, limited on one hand by its complete dependence on Russia for weaponry and economic support and on the other by its historical, traditional and cultural ties with China. In spite of the Russian aim of a unified Indochina to act as a buffer on China's southern flank (the Russian containment of China policy), the geophysical fact of Vietnam's vast northern neighbour can never be ignored. Russian support and pressure, however, might well have led, in addition to the absorption of Laos and Cambodia as semi-autonomous satellite states, to confrontation with China in northern Laos where the Chinese now have the dominant influence and are building a road through to the Thai border.

With an army after victory of high reputation and, on a combined population base of 40 millions, numbering not less than one million men, Thailand would have been the first to feel the heat through "competitive insurgency" promoted by China in the north and by Vietnam, as a Russian instrument, in the north-east. Others in South East Asia, with coasts accessible to arms supply by trawlers, would soon have followed. President Eisenhower's domino theory,* endorsed by all subsequent Presidents, is still accepted by South East Asian leaders in spite of the attempt by some wishful thinking American intellectuals to argue it under the mat. They cannot disprove it because only after the North's victory would it be put to the test.

All this spreading activity would have been described as "peaceful neutrality" which is defined as follows: "The peaceful neutrality proposed by our party is quite different from the neutralism of capitalism in a nationalistic country. Our neutrality is a new form of struggle and a part of the international proletarian revolution. Thus in reality there is no neutrality but the choice of the socialist side and the determination to fight back imperialism . . ."

A close second to the re-unification policy would have been "social transformation". The two in fact are linked together in all declarations. Here we get down to the heart of the matter — land reform, collectivisation and a bloodbath. It is here that the Westerner is completely confused because he is dealing with events beyond his imagination or the capacity of his mind to grasp.

Land reform, as carried out in North Vietnam, was not a programme but a pogrom. There was no agricultural nor administrative reason whatsoever for land reform since all land in North Vietnam was to be collectivised anyway, as it would be in the South. There was, however a political motive — to eliminate all persons potentially hostile to the party. The process was described by its manager, Truong Chinh, as "a tough political and ideological struggle to erase the

* See p. 166 below.

24

influence of hostile rightist and opportunistic ideas and revisionist ideologies from the mind of cadres and party members in order to safeguard the party, its line and its policy". Landlords and peasants were not the only target. Anyone could be denounced before the Peoples' Courts, even party members.

The purpose of collectivisation which followed the pogrom was to monopolise the livelihood open to each individual. All means of production were collectivised in North Vietnam so that nobody could opt out of the "socialist transformation" and everybody could be directed as to his occupation.

Although "grave mistakes" were admitted by all party leaders, the same pogrom would have been adopted in the South. This raises the question, if the invasion had succeeded and the North had taken over, what would the bloodbath have been? Looking at the record both in North Vietnam after 1954 and in South Vietnam during the course of the war, my own estimate is that it would not have been less than one million people (out of 19 millions). The reason for such a ruthless purge would have been that, if the North was to digest the South, it must eliminate all those who had played a positive part in the South's defence. There had been no mass uprising in support of the Vietcong or the NVA. The people of the South have been fighting to remain non-communist (which is why Hanoi can never accept a free internationally supervised election in the South as part of a settlement), but some, a good 5 per cent, are now fighting for actual survival for themselves and their families. The conqueror could not hope to hold and govern such a people without a bloodbath on a massive scale. We have the precedents in similar circumstances in Soviet Russia and China where the minimum figures are now put respectively at 20 millions and 34 millions. But in North Vietnam itself between 1946 and the peasants' revolt of 1956, the estimates are over 500,000 killed.

The International Control Commission, often quoted to dispute this figure, stated that it was not competent to investigate any charges of "reprisals" in the North after 1954 unless substantive proof was provided that the victims had been punished because of their ties with the former Government of Vietnam.[10] There was no investigation, and, therefore, no restraint.

As to what would have happened in the South, let us take the case of Hoi Thanh village in Tam Quan district in northern Binh Dinh where on 21 May this year [1972] a hamlet chief and 47 other villagers were buried alive after the area had been captured by the NVA 3 Division — and this is an area which most American journalists write off as being pro-VC. In that case what would have happened in the thousands of pro-GVN villages?

We have to accept the views of North Vietnamese defectors. Colonel Tran Van Dac, who defected after 24 years in the Communist party, stated that the communists, if they won, would slaughter up to 3 million South Vietnamese. Another Colonel, Le Xuyen Chuyen, who defected after 21 years, stated that 5 million people in South Vietnam were on the communist "blood-debt" list and that 10–15 per cent of these would pay with their lives. When asked in an interview if the possibility of a bloodbath had been exaggerated, he replied: "It could not be exaggerated. It will happen." When asked whether world opinion would deter it, he laughed and said: 'Who would be around to report it? It happened in North Vietnam and nobody cared. You Americans would not be here to see it. Once out, you would never come back. It would just happen. World opinion? It doesn't even grasp what is going on here right now."[11]

Distressing though the thought of a bloodbath may be, it is more disturbing to think as Douglas Pike, an expert on the Vietcong, expressed it: "The communists in Vietnam would create a silence. The world would call it peace" — and, I might add, would drift rudderless and inexorably into yet more dangerous war.

The article, by spelling out Hanoi's aims and intentions on the points requested by the *New York Times,* does as a consequence indicate the basic reasons why the people of South Vietnam are prepared to resist to the bitter end. It also by implication justified the policy of the United States (but not the strategy nor conduct of the war throughout) in helping the people of South Vietnam to resist. Unfortunately by quoting almost entirely from communist sources the argument was difficult to refute. No doubt the *New York Times* had hoped that I would have used sources, such as the American Administration, which could have been disparaged. It was no surprise, therefore, when on 13 September I received the following letter from the *New York Times*:

'With many apologies (but so many thanks for all your work on it) I regret we will not be publishing your article. We felt that your thinking, as exemplified in this piece, *did not fully carry out our proposed thesis* [sic]* so, while respecting your views, feel we cannot go ahead with publication.'

But they paid!

I regret that I do not know whether the Magazine published 'a more benign view of the probable outcome of the North's takeover' because I have the good fortune to live in an area where the *New York Times* is not available. This pleasant state, however, was once disturbed by a well-meaning friend who sent me the issue of 11 October, 1972, which contained Senator George McGovern's pre-election Vietnam peace proposals. The leading article excelled itself in distortion and emotion but was bereft of logic. Its main theme centred around Senator McGovern's 'unanswerable question': 'How can we really argue that it is good to accommodate ourselves to a billion Russian and Chinese communists but that we must somehow fight to the bitter end against a tiny band of peasant guerrillas in the jungles of little Vietnam?' That such a question could be put and then be regarded as unanswerable is unbelievable and almost frightening. The seeking of agreements to restrain the nuclear arms race and to reduce the size of conventional forces in Europe is hardly an accommodation when its underlying purpose is to impose limits on Russian and Chinese expansionist aims and thereby to prevent a confrontation or a miscalculation. Moreover, the unanswerable question suggests that the

* My italics.

attempt to reduce the greater threat to world peace can best be served by giving the lesser threat in Indochina a free run, whereas all historical experience teaches us that exactly the opposite is true. In any case, whatever interpretation is put on the word 'accommodation' it cannot be said that President Nixon was trying any less hard to reach a negotiated solution with North Vietnam on the war than he was with Russia and China on both that and other problems.

I also rather like the phrase 'tiny band of peasant guerrillas' to describe an army which had just carried out a massive conventional invasion with fourteen divisions and the most modern weaponry, which not one single country in the Western world other than the United States, given the shape and topography of South Vietnam, could have defeated alone without adequate outside air support—not even Israel. Senator McGovern's views also seem to suggest that he regards the 'little' as being of no importance. The more interesting question is: how big do you have to be not to be little? If measured by population (about forty-two millions for North and South) over a hundred members of the United Nations would fail to qualify. If measured by Army divisions (about thirty) even the United States would be little![12]

In the same issue there was also a letter to the Editor containing, amongst other things, the hoary misquotation of President Eisenhower about 80 per cent voting for Ho Chi Minh, which I have already dealt with, and also the fantasy that President Diem put a million people to death in the post-1954 period. The country would have been littered with corpses and yet there is not a scrap of evidence from any Vietnamese, any reporter, or any diplomat, who at that time could move freely round the country, to support such an absurd allegation, which many Americans were later happy to believe as an excuse for reneging on their commitment to South Vietnam. In Diem's suppression of the Binh Xuyen bandits, who controlled the vice rings of Saigon, in his attempt to curb the private armies of the Hoa Hao and Cao Dai sects, and in the pitched battles with Vietcong guerrillas, all of which were legitimate actions for a government, I doubt whether the number killed on all sides during the period of Diem's rule from 1954 to 1963 exceeded 100,000. Apart from these battle casualties (later in the war to be greatly exceeded) there were in addition 'political' prisoners and executions. I deal with the former in the next chapter, together with the more recent Phoenix programme. With regard to executions, I am quite sure that there were abuses but I would challenge any newly independent government in the Third World, which has suffered internal turbulence even to a lesser extent, to show a better record. President Diem certainly could not match the Vietcong. It was one reason for his loss of support that, when the Vietcong were murdering (i.e. in cold blood not in battle) an average of over 200 a month (and abducting more), including village and hamlet officials, their families and innocent members of the population, he failed to capture and execute the murderers and to protect the rural population.

It was during this period, when such accusations were made against Diem and obviously believed by some, that the North was indulging in its land reform pogrom in respect of which its leaders subsequently admitted 'grave mistakes'. Even General Giap, when detailing a long list of errors to the 10th Congress of the Party Central Committee, said: 'We made too many deviations and executed too many honest people. We attacked on too large a front and, seeing enemies everywhere, resorted to terror, which became far too widespread.' As one Vietnamese, Nguyen Manh Tuong, commented: 'The sacred principle applied to land reform was: it is better to kill ten innocent people than to let one enemy escape.' But this sort of terror, from which none could escape, worked. It enabled collectivization to follow, encouraged everyone to volunteer for any task and brought in taxes on demand. The admission of mistakes, or 'Rectification of Errors' campaign, which followed, promised such relief and respite that it was willingly misinterpreted as the sun shining again.

But the gem in the same October issue of the *New York Times* was the special article by Mr. James Reston in which he painfully argued to the point that 'surely there is something in between the President's policy of sticking with Thieu indefinitely and McGovern's policy of not only abandoning Thieu (and the people of South Vietnam) but wounding him on the way out'. The search for a correct middle policy is something to which Mr. James Reston might have addressed himself earlier. But this failure to apply intellect, compounded by distorted reporting, was a major feature of the war, which did much to destroy the objectivity of most of the American press (this deserves a book in itself which I hope will be written one day by a non-American).

Even the British press took its lead from this and I will merely quote two examples, out of hundreds, which stick in my mind. *The Sunday Times Magazine* on 17 September, 1972, had a glorious article on Cambodia before 1970 under Prince Sihanouk as a sort of Garden of Eden without a serpent. It curiously omitted the serpent altogether, although this was the dominant factor in the country at the time. The article failed to mention in its fulsome reporting that four North Vietnamese divisions were present in the country, that thousands of tons of military supplies were entering Sihanoukville in Russian and Chinese ships and were being transported to these divisions by the Hak Ly Truck Company from which Sihanouk himself was taking a fine rake-off! The other is more trivial, but is revealing of the malicious type of reporting to which Vietnam was always subject. In a critical piece on the Presidential election in Vietnam in October, 1971, *The Guardian* could not resist, as a result of a visit by its reporter to the largely Montagnard province of Pleiku, putting in a snide but telling snippet: 'And the Province Chief of Pleiku—a Vietnamese—says with enthusiasm: You see how democratic we Vietnamese are? We even give votes to these savages.' What the reporter must have known, whereas *The Guardian*'s readers did not, was that the Province Chief himself was, and had been for years, a Montagnard (Colonel Ya Ba, who was elected to the Senate in 1973).

But on the whole the British press, with the advantage of no British involvement and with considerable experience of similar circumstances, was the most objective. In this respect *The Economist* was outstanding and clearly understood the fundamental issues at every point in the war, but then it had its reputation to live up to as the world's best weekly. The French press, on the other hand, quite apart from being heavily penetrated, was influenced by pique and could not resist any opportunity to knock the Americans. It was therefore able to indulge its prejudice, and the French penchant for rumour and intrigue, which the Hanoi and NLF delegations to the peace talks adroitly manipulated. A favourite technique was to spread a rumour (for example, the bombing of the dykes) which no amount of denials could completely eradicate and which would generate its own momentum round the world press. This was not done solely for the purpose of the allegation itself. It also distracted attention from other issues, including counter-accusations which could be proved, such as the massacre of the hamlet chief and forty-seven villagers in northern Binh Dinh province. Such rumours helped to influence American policy decisions by increasing public pressure especially at a time when Hanoi itself was about to switch strategy, for example from invasion to an acceptance of the ceasefire offer. There is nowhere like the banks of the Seine for distilling a really smelly rumour. It was one of President Johnson's graver errors to select Paris for the peace talks. Warsaw would have been far better.

The main feature of the whole Western critical process was that it focused on American and South Vietnamese short-comings, which were readily apparent and undeniably many. They were used to show error of intention and failure of policy through the illogical argument that if the tyre bursts (and at times more than one burst) the car is no good. Admittedly on some occasions there was downright lying by 'official' spokes-men to improve their case, and on others serious misjudge-ments as to the real state of affairs. But none of these in themselves invalidated the policy. The press was right to show up these shortcomings, but this unfortunately led to a self-feeding confrontation between press and government which encouraged the press to neglect the shortcomings of the other side. These were mainly ignored or brushed aside. Rarely was any attention paid to North Vietnamese or Vietcong sources of information, i.e. what they were saying in captured documents, interro-gation reports, internal broadcasts and their official newspaper, *Nhan Dan*, as opposed to what they were saying for external consumption over Hanoi radio or in interviews to carefully selected visitors. This failure of research and balance created a comprehensibility rather than a credibility gap and went some way towards fulfilling President Diem's prophetic statement to me in 1962 that: 'Only the American press can lose this war.'

The lack of balance in reporting and the comprehensibility gap spilled over into the American academic community. One notable production which came my way was *The Indochina Story* by a Committee of Concerned Asian Scholars. It can best be described as no more than a gang bang on American post-war policy in South East Asia, and supports my view that one of the distressing results of the Vietnam war has been the degeneration of American scholarship in the current affairs field which later historians will hopefully rectify. Many of their arguments are indirectly answered by this book, but there is one point which needs to be specifically dealt with because it is a fundamental issue of the war.

One 'concerned scholar', after happily quoting me out of context, discussed what he called the 'fatal flaw' in counter-insurgency in the following terms: 'In reality, however, counter-insurgency is a social transformation on paper only; it has produced no revolutions in the third world. Quite the contrary, in fact. . . . Its accomplishments are at best negative. As in Malaya, it may prevent a revolutionary takeover but, having done that, the desire for a social transformation disappears and reforms are dropped. . . . Social change, like refugee camps and free fire-zones, is only a means employed for gaining control, it is not the end in itself. Though it speaks of transformation, an anti-guerrilla operation always stops short of meaningful change. It is a "success" that one should not want to inflict on the peoples of the third world.'

That is a load of tripe, as any visitor to Singapore and Malaya can tell you. Now, in the 1970s, it is hard to realize that, up to ten years ago, the peoples of these two countries and their present elected leaders were fighting for survival against, and achieving decisive victories over, the Malayan Communist Party with, thanks to counter-insurgency, surprisingly little damage and comparatively little loss of life. The subsequent remarkable changes, not least in prosperity, health and social services, over the last ten years or more give the lie to the fashionable sociological theory that counter-insurgency is basically reactionary because its aim is to restore or maintain the social status quo. No status quo, especially not the social, can be maintained through a long period of violence. The energy generated in both a government and people during an insurgency cannot suddenly be turned off like a tap when it is over. It naturally spills over into other fields, such as development, which continue to produce sweeping changes. This is very evident in Singapore and Malaya, and stems from the MCP threat. In any case, during the Malayan Emergency the status quo was never an aim, implicit or explicit, in the policy of successive British and Malayan governments, nor in the minds of those who carried it out. The aim in this respect has been most succinctly expressed by Sir Winston Churchill, though in an earlier context, as 'ordered unceasing change and progress'.[13] I still believe that orderly change is a fundamental desire of the human race in every continent and every walk of life, even more so in those countries which have suffered turbulent transitions to independence with long periods of violence either before, during or after changes in political power.

The theory of the 'concerned scholar' rests mainly on the assumption that the choice lies only between colonialism or an authoritarian regime on the one hand and revolutionary nationalism or communism on the other and that, given only this choice, the people will opt for the latter. As far as it goes this may be true and is supported by that statement of President Eisenhower's already quoted. But in South Vietnam, as often elsewhere, these were not the only choices. Ngo Dinh Diem on his return from exile offered a nationalist alternative which received widespread popular support. The disillusion with Diem's subsequent performance under Vietcong insurgency pressure in no way affected the basic popular search for such an alternative. Even if under subsequent governments up to President Thieu the alternative was only partly achieved, at least the possibility of the alternative was kept open, whereas under Ho Chi Minh and his successors it would have gone for ever. It is only necessary to compare Malaya and Singapore today, where the alternative was found, with North Vietnam where it never will be. The latter is probably, as a Stalinist hangover, the most repressive and reactionary regime in the world, with the lowest prospect of progress in any field and with less individual freedom than an ant in an antheap. In considering social change therefore as an important factor in determining choice, it is a patent error to suppose that, given any other alternative, the people will choose communism.

It is an even greater error when the choice of communism is justified, by such neo-scholars as Miss Frances Fitzgerald in her book *The Fire in the Lake*, on the ground that totalitarianism is good for the natives or the only form of government they understand. She did not adopt, in addition, an exactly scholarly approach to her research. Referring to the strategic hamlet programme in 1962 she stated:

'In its very conception the programme was a study in misplaced analogy. Sir Robert Thompson, the head of the British team of advisers to Ngo Dinh Diem, proposed to build up a system of fortified villages such as the British had used against the Communist insurgency in Malaya. The difficulty was that while in Malaya the British had fortified Malay villages against Chinese insurgents, in Vietnam the Vietnamese would have to fortify Vietnamese hamlets against other Vietnamese who had grown up in those hamlets.'

I cannot recollect any 'new villages', as fortified villages were called in Malaya, which were predominantly Malay, but out of over 500 there just might have been one. Otherwise all the new villages were Chinese, with the great majority almost one hundred per cent Chinese, some of whom supported the insurgents; so that in that aspect the analogy was hardly 'misplaced'.

For her edification the fortified, or 'combat' hamlet (ap chien dau) was a communist concept used originally by the Vietminh and later the Vietcong to protect hamlets in remote rural areas under their control. It was copied by President Diem (as were other communist methods) and was incorporated into the strategic hamlet (ap chien luoc) programme for the defence of hamlets in contested areas. This programme was already under way before the British Advisory Mission arrived in Vietnam in

1961. In fact in the province of Ninh Tuan, when I first visited it, the programme was almost completed. What the British Advisory Mission tried to inject was strategic control of the programme through priorities, including allocation of resources, co-ordination of supporting forces, a simple organizational structure and all the other ingredients necessary to make the programme work. Although it failed in 1960–64, it at least worried the Vietcong into admitting in captured documents that 1962 was the only year in which they made no progress. The lessons of this earlier period and of later abortive attempts were learnt, and the programme worked admirably from 1969 to 1971 under the title 'Pacification'. Fortunately a superb account has been written of a village[14] (not far from My Lai) moving from Vietcong domination to a contested situation and finally to a successful 'strategic hamlet' defended by its own people. There were incidentally, plenty of fortified hamlets about in 1973 on both sides after the ceasefire. The depth and accuracy of Miss Fitzgerald's research on this point was matched by others. As the review in *The Times Literary Supplement*[15] kindly pointed out: 'Her criterion when choosing sources seems to be whether they support the thesis she is urging rather than whether their authors were in any position to know.'

The canting and ranting of others on the subject of American atrocities were more than adequately dealt with in an article on the *Propaganda of Atrocity* in the London *Times* by Robert Conquest on 12 January, 1972. Miss Mary McCarthy was one of those at that time who could see only the American aberrations but never the intentional terrorism of the other side. She actually had the effrontery to state on a BBC programme that there was no verifiable evidence of atrocities committed by the NVA or the Vietcong against women and children. I deal with such atrocities in the next chapter and it is not for me to discourage Miss McCarthy from holding views which do not take into account facts which any serious person with a little time and trouble could verify. She, and those like her, must find little comfort in the superb article by Alexander Solzhenitsyn on Peace and Violence[16] which attacks the West for its moral cowardice and double standards.

Solzhenitsyn first makes the distinction, not between peace and war but between peace and violence, which are equally indivisible, whereas war is not; it is merely a noisier form of violence. Being anti-war therefore is not enough, and he points to the striking fact that the United Nations 'cannot even succeed in carrying through a moral condemnation of terrorism'. He flippantly proposes as a definition of terrorism: 'When we are attacked, that is terrorism; when we do the attacking, that is a partisan freedom movement.' More seriously he states that 'we refuse to recognise as terrorism a treacherous attack in time of peace against peaceful people by militia, secretly armed and often in civilian clothes'. We are then called upon to study their objectives and to recognize them as dedicated guerrillas. Terrorism passes over into guerrilla activity and then into conventional war across frontiers. 'Certain problems about classification can be posed especially for those who have an emotional interest in not getting at the truth, but in justifying one form or another of violence.'

'The error . . . is an emotional error. We do not make a mistake because it is difficult to perceive the truth. It even lies on the surface, but we make a mistake because it is more comfortable.' He obviously had the Vietnam war in mind because he goes on:

'The proven brutal mass murders in Hue are only noted in passing, almost immediately pardoned, because society's sympathy inclined to that view point, and no one wanted to go against this inertia. It was nothing short of scandalous that these accounts leaked out in the free press and for a (very short) time caused (precious little) embarrassment to the frenetic defenders of that social system. Can one really believe that the little fluttering butterfly Ramsey Clark, nevertheless previously Minister of Justice [Attorney-General] quite simply "could not understand", quite simply could not guess, that the prisoner of war who hands him a paper essential for an obviously political purpose, has first been submitted to torture?'

With regard to Czechoslovakia, as compared with Rhodesia, he could not resist adding (nor can I):

'It was with the same moral grimacing that the British

Leader of the Labour Party was able to screw up his courage and go to another country (not an African country, of course, he would never have been allowed to do that!), and there issue arbitrary "pardons" to the regime without consulting the local population.'

He gets to the heart of the matter when he refers to the Australian and New Zealand protests at the French nuclear tests but not against the more serious Chinese ones. He then gives the reason: 'Not only because of a moral grimace but quite simply because of cowardice. Because from an expedition into the Chinese desert or along the Chinese coast no one would return—and they know it. It is the hypocrisy of the West that protests are only made when there is no danger, when the opposition is likely to capitulate and when the protester is safe from being censured by the leftist circle.'

I have no doubt at all, if North Vietnam was finally to win, it would be invaded by carriers of free pardons and curriers of cheap favours. All would be conveniently forgiven or forgotten. It is only right and proper that those who indulge in these double standards should be rebuked by a respected Russian dissident and a Nobel Prize winner for Literature.

CHAPTER III

MYTHS, REALITIES AND IRRELEVANCES

Television was to play at least an equal part with the press in influencing opinion on the war. For the first time the horrors of war were brought into the sitting room and it has been tritely said that the British would have lost the Boer war on television. I have discussed the problems and shortcomings of television with many people. The camera has a more limited view even than the cameraman and argues always from the particular to the general. If on television one child is shown to be scarred by napalm then every child has been scarred by napalm. If one house is destroyed then all houses are destroyed. If a police chief shoots one prisoner then all prisoners are shot. The proof of one —the camera does not lie—is proof for all. Moreover the director and crew naturally want the more spectacular shots, and in war the most spectacular picture is that of destruction. The camera must go where that sort of action is. All activity of a less spectacular nature, even though constructive and more important, is neglected. This inevitably leads to distortion and lack of balance. It even becomes false when small rent-a-crowd rioters arrange a rendezvous and wait for the cameras to arrive before starting. After one such 'riot' in Saigon in support of Air Vice-Marshal Ky's Presidential candidacy, in which about 200 people were involved, a former member of the British Labour Government who was there to cover the election asked: 'What are the other two million people in Saigon doing?' The camera did not answer that.

The point is that every allegation ever made about South Vietnam can probably be proved at least in one instance. It could be equally proved about the other side if access could have been gained to the material or event. There is no issue in this world in which we are dealing with the darkest black on one side and the purest white on the other. What is necessary is to differentiate between the lighter and darker shades of grey. In this respect, if President Diem made the more prophetic

38

statement about the press, Dr. Henry Kissinger certainly made the more perceptive judgement: 'The dilemma is that almost any statement about Vietnam is likely to be true; unfortunately, truth does not guarantee relevance.'[17]

The massacre at My Lai was abhorrent and inexcusable and yet, when it was revealed, it did not surprise me. In the tensions of war there will always be aberrations, however high the general character and standards of behaviour of the country concerned, when millions of its citizens are involved as soldiers. I would defy any country to claim otherwise. Given a combination of circumstances—intense provocation, frustration, inexperience, lack of superior direct supervision and control, anxiety as to either survival or performance and, not least, lack of intelligence—something like a My Lai will happen whatever the safeguards. My Lai was an irredeemable blemish on the American record but, like most of the South Vietnamese to whom I have talked, I do not hold it against them. Nor does it in any way alter the issues of the war. It was both out of character and contrary to orders, in so far as such acts can ever be forbidden by instruction. That this was so was clearly shown by the number of those present who refused to take part in it and others who did their utmost to stop it.

The same cannot be said for the other side. There was no equivalent reporting of Vietcong or North Vietnamese atrocities, which occurred on a scale which makes My Lai almost insignificant. Everyone heard of My Lai, but who heard of Cai Be where the Vietcong, after its capture, lingered only to murder forty wives and children of the local militia company, or of the Montagnard village of Dak Son where they moved from hut to hut with flame throwers incinerating more than 250 villagers, two-thirds of them women and children? Most people have heard of the massacres at Hue in 1968, where the Vietcong and North Vietnamese executed about 5,700 people (as assessed from the mass graves found afterwards in the sand dunes outside the town). But who knows that in captured documents they gloated over these figures and only complained that they had not killed enough? But, in many ways, because of the terror inspired, the continual individual assassinations in the villages averaging thousands a year throughout the war were worse.

One of the nastiest to come to my attention, in Long An province south of Saigon, was when a small mixed squad of Vietcong and NVA called an old man out of his house and demanded that he write to all six of his sons, who were serving in the government forces, calling on them to defect. He absolutely refused and turned round to re-enter his house. They put a burst of AK 47 into his back.[18] Do you wonder that villagers are prepared to fight or that ARVN infantry battalions in 1973 were over 600 strong? All these acts were not aberrations, accidents or errors of aim, but part of a ruthless calculated policy designed to break a people who would not otherwise bend to the communist will.

The world cannot plead ignorance, because this policy has been well documented by Dr. Stephen Hosmer in a book on Vietcong Repression ('Repression' is the Vietcong's own word for it). The evidence and documentation were taken almost exclusively from North Vietnamese and Vietcong sources. Perhaps, because it did not quote Senator McGovern as the leading least-knowledgeable authority, the book received little public attention. The evidence has been further authoritatively put together in a compendium entitled 'The Human Cost of Communism in Vietnam' prepared, somewhat surprisingly, for the United States Senate Committee on the Judiciary by Senator James Eastland,[19] and not by Senator J. W. Fulbright and the Foreign Affairs Committee.

Bombing by the United States Air Force created even more of a trauma. Much has been made of the fact that over 7,500,000 tons of bombs, over five million more than were dropped by the United States in World War II, have been dropped in Indochina. This gives the impression that the countryside has been ravaged, that most towns and villages have ceased to exist, and that the civilian casualties must have been enormous. But the main weight of these bombs in South Vietnam was dropped in uninhabited jungle or swamp areas along the infiltration routes, and at those points where the major battles, as a result of that infiltration, were fought. Some such areas must have been bombed at least 100 times. By the very nature of the country and terrain the damage and casualties have been light as compared with those of World War II. When in 1970 I raised in Washington the problem of reconstruction, hands were held up in horror at the likely cost. I hastened to add that the cost would be negligible in terms of the aid levels then being discussed; that the only asset almost irreparably damaged, and that not by bombing but by Vietcong action, was the north–south railway line from Saigon to Hue, and that this was no longer required socially, administratively or militarily in view of the new highway and coastal traffic. Given a real peace the outward scars of the war in the South would disappear within a year. Traces of the damage caused by the Tet offensive in the towns would now be hard to find. In 1970 and 1971 I flew over and visited many areas where there had been frequent fighting in the 1960s and where, except perhaps for a burnt-out truck on the roadside or a demolished railway bridge, you would hardly have known that there had been a war.[20]

The same may not be true in North Vietnam, where the bombing was directed specifically on the war-making infrastructure and communications with some considerable effect. At a time when Hanoi was complaining of its six civilian casualties, as a result of the first American raid on the North in April after the 1972 invasion began, its own troops were firing 122mm rockets indiscriminately into Saigon and Phnom Penh killing more than ten times that number. Over 70,000 rounds of mortar and artillery were fired into An Loc during the siege, pounding it to rubble (7,000 rounds were fired in one night) and over 1,100 civilians were killed. The NVA's 130mm Russian guns did much the same to Kontum and Quang Tri. When the civilian population fled from the latter there followed, in the words of a British war correspondent 'an act of calculated butchery unprecedented even in this conflict. Forward observers for the communist artillery targeted the columns of desperate refugees. They blasted them on the roads and in the fields, whether they travelled by truck, car, bicycle or on foot.'[21] The world was not intended to see this but it was revealed in all its horror when Quang Tri was later recaptured. The casualties along Route 1 (the stretch of road is now known as 'La Route Terrible') were estimated at over 20,000. I regret that I am not one of those who subscribes to the view that atrocities committed by shells and bullets in this way are all good clean civilised fun, whereas only casualties inflicted by bombs are evil. I might add that, as a result of these acts, I have had no moral qualms whatsoever about the bombing of the North, both as a retaliation and as a legitimate act of war.

From its very outset, the war created refugees and South Vietnam has had a remarkable record in coping with them. Over 800,000 left the North in 1954 after the Geneva settlement, and this figure would probably have been greater if the International Control Commission teams had not been prevented from making contact with further groups, or if the time period of 300 days during which such movement was allowed had been extended. But the North, like East Germany, could not tolerate such an exodus. These refugees were all resettled, mainly in their village groupings, in the South and established prosperous land settlements which they have defended valiantly ever since against the Vietcong and North Vietnamese invaders. A further 250,000 Vietnamese who fled from Cambodia in 1970 were also absorbed without noticeable effort. The great majority of the 3 million or more who had fled from the countryside into the local towns in the years between 1959 and 1969 were subsequently resettled back in their villages under the pacification programme before the 1972 invasion began. That in turn generated a further 750,000 who fled before the invader, more than half of them from Quang Tri and other districts north of Hue. Somehow, with American relief assistance, the South Vietnamese managed to cope even in the midst of war. It was estimated in 1973 that there were still about 500,000 refugees who may not be able or may not want to return to their villages which are in NVA hands. There has been a tendency by the critics to inflate these figures and Jane Fonda, for example, was still talking in 1972 in terms of 4 millions. One point not widely recognized is that there are two other movements of people occurring which have little or no connection with the war. Even within South Vietnam the Nam Tien, or advance southward, is still going on and there are movements of people from the densely populated coastal plains of central Vietnam to the Delta where land is still available. Also, in common with the rest of Asia, there is also a steady movement from the countryside to the towns. I can remember, when the first refugee camps were being established on the outskirts of towns, recommending that they should be planned as permanent suburbs because, even though the refugees first filling them might later return to their villages, this natural movement of people together with the population explosion would continue to fill them.

It has not gone unnoticed that the refugees always fled to the South and away from Vietcong or North Vietnamese control. The suggestion that the refugees preferred the South to the North was quite unacceptable to the critics, who put forward the theory that they were fleeing from American bombing. Yet, in 1940, when Belgians, Dutch and the people of northern France fled westward there was no American bombing and practically no Allied bombing. If they were fleeing from the German Stukas, they were fleeing along the routes likely to be subject to further attacks. I cannot believe that these refugees were very different from the South Vietnamese. They fled towards the side with which they were identified and from which they expected succour and the better treatment.

Finally, while on the subject of bombing, the dykes must be mentioned. In the Red River Delta, as in the Mekong Delta and elsewhere in Vietnam, there are thousands of miles of canals, large and small, for drainage, irrigation and communications. Moreover, in areas where land is only just above sea level, the best way to obtain the raised foundations for a road or railway is to dig a canal first alongside. In the attacks on the road and rail communication system in the North such irrigation canals were inevitably damaged by bombing, just as they were in the South by similar North Vietnamese attacks on communications there. But these irrigation works are not 'the dykes'. The Red River over many centuries has been steadily silting up, with the result that its present bed is now in some places six feet higher than the surrounding countryside. Instead of its bed being dredged, the banks have been constantly raised and in many areas are now more than 40 feet high. In periods of heavy flood they are frequently breached and need constant maintenance and repair. If they were to burst, the whole Red River Delta round Hanoi would be inundated. It is questionable whether, except in the area of the breach, there would be serious loss of life because the area of spread for the water is enormous. But there would be much damage to property and the annual rice crop might be lost. All through the summer of 1972 there were constant allegations that the United States Air Force was bombing the dykes. The answer to that allegation is that, if 'smart' bombs had been used on the dykes, they would have been breached in twenty-four hours. Hanoi and the whole surrounding countryside would have been under two to three feet of water. It is interesting to note that, as time went on and this did not occur, these allegations were quietly dropped. Nevertheless the threat of bombing the dykes is a major factor which must always give Hanoi cause for concern.

After atrocities and the bombing, perhaps the greatest controversy raged over the question of 'political prisoners'. There have been consistent allegations that the number of political prisoners held in the South was as high as 200,000, though the figure more frequently banded about was 100,000. When distortion and misrepresentation are the names of the game it is not surprising that such figures were rounded up and then doubled or trebled. Moreover, no distinction was drawn between prisoners of war (nearly 27,000 with which I deal later), normal criminal offenders, those sentenced for a particular terrorist act and those detained as suspected supporters of the Vietcong or North Vietnamese invader, and therefore as a security threat to the state. Between 1968 and the end of 1972 the total figures for these last three categories, excluding POWs, averaged just over 30,000. The lowest figure was 27,570 in February, 1972, before the invasion, and the highest figure was 39,790 in November, 1972, after the invasion. In the totals of these four years the normal criminal element averaged about one-third and the two communist elements (those convicted of terrorist acts or suspected supporters) were about two-thirds. Out of a total population by 1972 of about 19 millions only ·21 per cent (the highest figure of 39,790) were under investigation, detained or sentenced for all causes. Excluding the ·09 per cent of normal criminals, the two communist elements were just less than ·12 per cent of the population.[22] These can be divided into three parts: suspects under investigation (under 4,000) including those released before trial; those tried and sentenced (over 14,000) by a provincial tribunal, consisting of the Province Chief and elected provincial representatives, to detention for periods from six months to a maximum of two years (this procedure required a minimum of three separate sources of information against each prisoner — compare Eire where the word of a Superintendent of Police is enough to get a member of the IRA held for six months); and those tried and sentenced (about 4,500) by a military court for actual offences, up to and including murder, with the more serious (2,000–2,500) receiving sentences of over five years.

It is interesting to make some comparisons. With regard to normal criminals (·09 per cent of the population in South Vietnam in November, 1972) the figures on 28 October, 1972, for the free peaceful state of Massachusetts were 4,945 out of a population of 5·8 millions, i.e. ·085 per cent, or almost exactly the same. With regard to the communist elements sentenced or detained (·12 per cent of the population in South Vietnam) the highest figure at one time in Malaya was over 10,000 out of a population of about 7 millions, i.e. ·14 per cent or higher than in Vietnam. The figures for Vietnam cannot therefore be regarded as extraordinary or excessive.

Nevertheless, the controversy over 'political prisoners' does raise the whole question of detention and the procedures for it during an insurgency and, it should not be forgotten, an invasion. Detention may be repugnant to those brought up in the British tradition of justice, under which in normal times a person should only be confined if remanded by a magistrate, sentenced by a court after a fair trial or certified insane. Nevertheless, in time of declared war, in undeclared or civil wars or in periods of extreme political violence amounting to an emergency, detention is recognized as a powerful weapon in a government's armoury and has always been used. Many countries have included it in statute law for use whether an emergency is declared or not, while other countries may require the declaration of an emergency before regulations authorizing detention can come into force. Procedures and the treatment of detainees will largely hinge on the case for, and the intention of, detention itself in the circumstances of the time.

In time of declared war hundreds of thousands are liable to be detained either under the rules of war or by executive act under war-time regulations. Prisoners of war are held (in some, but not all,[23] recent cases under conditions laid down by the Geneva Conventions) to prevent them fighting again and such detention is a humane alternative to their being killed or enslaved as in earlier times. Enemy civilians are also interned for the duration of the war, not necessarily for anything which they may have done, but to prevent them committing any hostile act. In a declared war, such as World War II, the threat to a country, its people and territory, its government and constitution and its very survival is so apparent that no one questions such detention. Even citizens of the country itself who have committed no treasonable act but are considered to sympathize with the enemy may be detained. National emotion, coupled with inadequate security intelligence, may even dictate that more are detained as security risks than is strictly necessary as, for example, in the case of Americans of Japanese origin after Pearl Harbour.

Even enemy civilians in their own country, if not in uniform and not members of a recognized military unit, who commit hostile acts such as firing on the occupying forces may be treated as *franc tireurs*. Guerrillas or members of a resistance movement captured in civilian clothes have few rights under the rules of war. They can be summarily tried and shot. To treat them as prisoners of war and detain them is a humanitarian (but more frequently a political) consideration. There is therefore in a declared war still some uncertainty as to a captured civilian's status and treatment. In undeclared wars, many of which are bitter civil wars sometimes with racial or religious undertones, or in periods of extreme political violence, the problem is greater. It can be further complicated by the involvement of aliens or outsiders on both sides. This has not made it easy for governments to decide with any precision when persons should be charged before the courts, treated as prisoners of war or otherwise detained.

When a ruthless terrorist organization is involved on one side, the problem of charging a person in court is obvious. Witnesses take the stand at the risk of their lives. Indeed, from the government point of view, the mere attempt to charge a terrorist in court may be tantamount to sentencing the probable witnesses and members of their families to death. Even if an impartial jury could be found its members would almost certainly be intimidated and in some cases the judge also. Moreover, some of the sources of evidence may be delicate from the intelligence point of view and require to be safeguarded, as being of more value in the future rather than being blown to secure one conviction. To some extent the problem can be solved by making it a criminal offence to be caught in certain circumstances where only the factual evidence at the time of arrest is enough to secure a conviction; for example, by defining a terrorist as a person carrying arms, ammunition or explosives without a licence. Breaking a curfew and carrying food or other listed articles in a prohibited area can also be made offences which require only factual evidence to be given by members of the security forces arresting the individual. Heavy penalties can be imposed and, in fact, in Malaya during the Emergency any person charged with carrying arms, and thereby being defined as a terrorist, was subject on conviction to a mandatory death penalty. Such harsh laws, however, have to be used sparingly and chiefly against hard-core terrorists known to have committed bestial acts against the civilian population. The point here is that a government must be seeking eventual reconciliation with the main body of terrorist supporters. This is unlikely to be achieved by a policy of wholesale revenge through hangings and heavy prison sentences as a result of charges in court. On the other hand, captured or arrested terrorists and their active supporters cannot be immediately released. They therefore have to be detained until such time as they can be safely released to become law-abiding citizens again. Detention therefore should be regarded as less drastic than being charged in court, and is really equivalent to being treated as a prisoner of war without being accorded that formal status.

Basically the primary purpose of detention is to prevent people who by their specific acts, behaviour and associations represent a threat to the country similar to an enemy in war through their intention to carry out, or to support those carrying out, violent hostile acts. A citizen is just as much entitled to protection from hand grenades in a bar or bombs in a street as from a land mine dropped from a German aircraft. If captured, the crew of that aircraft would be detained for the duration. Similarly in undeclared war or conditions of extreme political violence designed to effect political and constitutional changes by force some form of detention is essential. It should be accepted that these are wars, at least in Mao Tse Tung's sense that war is 'politics with bloodshed', or in Solzhenitsyn's sense that any act of violence is a violation of peace. Those captured or arrested by the security forces, or who surrender, should be detained like prisoners of war but without that status and without prejudice to their being subsequently charged in court for any criminal act equivalent to a war crime.

The decision whether to charge in court or whether to detain is an executive act, as is any order of detention itself which is made under powers approved by the legislature. Detention is not a judicial act. It should not even be a semi-judicial act because it is quite improper to put courts in a position where they have to assess a security risk and order detention or release. Detention is not a sentence. The original order may be for a certain period but it can be reviewed or renewed on the merits of each case. If any procedure is adopted which takes detention out of the hands of the executive, then it may place an intolerable strain on the security forces if it proves to be too inconsistent or lenient. Under extreme provocation they may not be prepared to arrest an individual for the second or third time. Trying to shelter behind the judiciary or a special court, or leaving the security forces in doubt, represents a failure on the part of a government to grasp the nettle firmly.

The whole tone of the government's treatment for those under detention will be set by whether or not it has a clearly defined surrender policy, which should not be a running amnesty forgiving any crime, even those not yet committed. Moreover, those who willingly surrender are one of the best sources of information. This policy is an essential feature for the ultimate aim of reconciliation. A successful policy will depend almost entirely on the treatment not only of those who surrender but also of those who are captured or arrested, because the distinction can easily be blurred by terrorist propaganda. The mere fact that such propaganda has to be put out by the other side, and other more brutal measures taken (such as executing those suspected of wanting to surrender), is evidence that the surrender policy is hurting and weakening the terrorist grip. This general approach by the government, quite apart from moral considerations, eliminates any question of torture or harsh treatment as being completely counter-productive.

No one would pretend that detention procedures anywhere are foolproof and do not lead to abuses and to innocent persons being detained. The GVN tried to reduce this risk by introducing the 'An Tri' procedure, under which individuals had to be brought before a provincial tribunal and sentenced. In my view this was a mistake, as it led to the further unfortunate situation that many of the worst terrorists received only the maximum sentence of two years, after which they were released again into the population. Nevertheless, considering the whole circumstances of the war, the procedures and the treatment were better than might have been expected and bore no comparison with the disgraceful treatment of civilian and military prisoners (when taken) held by the Vietcong,[24] and of American POWs held by the North Vietnamese. In this last respect the treatment of captured NVA and VC held as POWs by South Vietnam was strictly in accordance with the Geneva Conventions including inspection by the Red Cross. The criticism directed at the South on this whole question of 'political prisoners' might have been less shrill if comparisons had been made and if the humiliating treatment accorded to American POWs had been known earlier.

In relation both to atrocities and to detention the subject which came in for the greatest criticism was the Phoenix programme. This was categorized as a programme designed to counter terror with terror, particularly by the use of assassination. This whole subject was very ably dealt with by Ambassador William Colby in his evidence before a Congressional Committee.[25] In answer to a specific question on the counter-terror point he replied:

'The Phoenix programme does not combat Communist terror with terror. It identifies members of the Viet Cong infrastructure for apprehension and detention according to Vietnamese law. My opening statement and testimony, I believe, explains the circumstances in which VCI are killed in the course of military operations or fighting off apprehension, and places in perspective such unjustifiable abuses as have occurred. This does not constitute fighting Communist terror with terror.'

In previous writings I have always argued very strongly against the use of terror or torture or indeed of any act not sanctioned by law. A government, however, cannot allow its officials and citizens to be murdered and terrorized without taking measures both to protect the population against further such attacks and to apprehend those responsible. To achieve this last requires a good intelligence organization, with some of the attributes of a CID (or homicide department), designed to identify the individuals and their accomplices. At one time (in 1966) I counted in the Saigon area alone seventeen separate American and South Vietnamese intelligence organizations, many of which had this as one of their tasks. Phoenix was therefore less a programme, because the task already existed, than an attempt on the part of the GVN to co-ordinate its various intelligence services and sources, especially at the district and province levels, and to improve procedures for the maintenance of dossiers and for the apprehension of members of the Vietcong infrastructure thus identified. In so far as it was a programme, this re-organization helped to focus attention on the need to target members of the underground political organization of the Vietcong in addition to its military units. It was not always easy to differentiate between the two because, in some cases, many individuals were in both and wore two hats, and because, as pacification advanced, the great majority of the VCI left the populated areas and operated with local guerrilla units. Some of the higher ranking ones, at Province Committee level, even left the country and operated from Cambodia. Although such individuals were classified as political, they were either armed themselves or moved with armed units or bodyguards. The few who remained inside the population, while they may have had access to arms when required, moved without them when there was a risk of meeting village defence force patrols or of passing a check-point. Generally, when in or close to government controlled areas, those outside, who had to maintain contact with the population, and the VCI in the population, who had to maintain contact with units outside, moved at night. There was still plenty of activity round the villages from 1969 to 1971. The figure for VC terrorist incidents for this period up to May, 1971, was 26,732 as a result of which 14,518 civilians were killed, 32,363 wounded and 16,226 abducted.

This meant that there were thousands of small-scale exchanges of fire in which members of the VCI were killed or captured, the great majority of which were not originated as a Phoenix operation and some of which were not even initiated by the government forces but by the Vietcong or NVA. Nevertheless, if a member of the VCI was accounted for, the credit was given to Phoenix in order to meet the target quotas set for each Province annually by the GVN. This quota system led to the further situation where individuals who had been killed or captured, were subsequently claimed as VCI although they were not on record as such before the action took place. During the period 1968 to May, 1971, Phoenix claimed a total of 67,282 VCI, of which 20,527 were killed; 17,717 rallied (surrendered); and 28,978 were captured (and subsequently convicted, detained or released). Of those killed it was carefully checked for 1970 and 1971 that over 87 per cent were killed in normal exchanges of fire and that the remainder were killed in action with the Police, including Special Branch, the Police Field Force (light infantry platoons) or the Police Reconnaissance Units (squads), not necessarily in a Phoenix-initiated operation. In fact, I made frequent inquiries on this point during this period and found that there were very few operations targeted against a specific member of the VC mainly because, while his identity might be established, not sufficient was known of his whereabouts or *modus operandi*. Many of them were killed in random ambushes during curfew hours at night. But, of course, there were some who were targeted and killed in the attempt to capture them. Now I am not prepared to say, nor would anyone, that some of those killed might have been captured or may have been summarily shot after capture. In a war of this nature, where individual animosities run very high indeed, that is bound to happen; but it was not the intention or the fault of the Phoenix programme and would have happened irrespective of the programme. If the killings by the Vietcong had been limited to a few similar such incidents (and to exchanges of fire in battle), they equally could not have been accused of conducting a terrorist campaign.

A further criticism was raised as to whether members of the VCI were entitled to POW status, or whether they could be detained without being sentenced by a court in view of the Geneva Conventions of 1949 (to which North Vietnam did not adhere while the South accepted them). The answers to these legal questions are perfectly clear. With regard to POW status, Article 4 of the Third Convention of 1949 on protection of POWs lays down certain standards for recognition of POWs. In Vietnam, both the United States and the GVN, as a conscious policy, went beyond these and accorded POW status to thousands of paramilitary and other persons captured who were not entitled to it under the Convention. A member of the VCI is not entitled to that status by this Article and was not normally accorded it. With regard to detention, Article 4 of the Fourth Convention on protection of civilian persons in time of war provides that persons protected by that convention are those who find themselves in the hands of a party to the conflict, or occupying power, of which they are not nationals. This means that civilians detained by their own government are not covered by the Article. The only party in the Vietnam war which could break this Article was the North Vietnamese Army—and did, intentionally, as a matter of policy, notably in Binh Dinh province during the 1972 invasion as described later.*

One measure of the success of Phoenix was that, during the 1972 invasion, there was not, as far as I am aware, one single VC incident of any consequence in the whole city of Saigon. This does not say much for the prospects of urban guerrillas when such a sprawling city swollen by refugees should have

* See p. 108.

been ideal for them. Or could it be that support for the government was rather more than the ten to fifteen per cent to which the critics of the GVN were prepared to testify? Of course, after the Ceasefire Agreement, Phoenix ceased to exist, but terrorist incidents in the countryside continued almost unabated right through 1973 even after the second Ceasefire Agreement (known as the Joint Communiqué) in June. Apart from individual assassinations there were hand grenades thrown into crowded places, including pagodas and schools, and explosive charges detonated without warning. I will quote two for Miss McCarthy to verify. On the evening of 10 September, 1973, VC detonated a bomb in a crowd of people at Tho Lac hamlet (Pho Dai village, Duc Pho District, Quang Ngai Province) killing three villagers, the projectionist and a PF soldier and wounding twenty-two. On the night of 13 September, 1973, the children of Duy Xuyen primary school were watching their classmates present songs and dramatic skits. A bomb detonated by the VC killed 8 children and wounded 24, including 12 children and 10 parents.[26] All such terrorist acts are expressly forbidden by Article 3 of the Ceasefire Agreement. Their perpetrators, whether NVA or VC, whether civilian or military, can be charged with murder under the normal criminal code of the country. It is the task of the Police, aided by the armed forces, to hunt them down. There is no longer a need to regard any crime as 'political' or to treat the criminal committing it as a 'political prisoner'.

Perhaps the most ridiculous outcry was that directed against the 'tiger cages' in the penal settlement on Con Son Island. Although the buildings dated from the French period before World War II, this settlement, being an island, was able to allow unusual freedom of movement to prisoners. They were employed throughout the island on public works. They could keep vegetable gardens, pigs and poultry and could fish in the sea, all of which helped to supplement their rations. Naturally in every prison, for disciplinary purposes, there have to be solitary confinement cells. These were the 'tiger cages', with bars down part of the door and along the top of each cell beneath a higher roof. They were not underground as implied by the carefully angled photographs which were taken. Suffice it to say that, as a result of the outcry, these have now been replaced by cells on the American model, i.e. with a concrete roof and ventilation solely through the bars on the door. In a tropical climate these are ovens, but no doubt that is what the agitators wanted. One block of 'tiger cages' was preserved for comparison and was subsequently taken over by militia families as the coolest accommodation on the island! I can only hope that, for the sake of the prisoners, the new solitary confinement cells will eventually be converted back into 'tiger cages'. As a result of the outcry which naturally encouraged indiscipline amongst the prisoners, all privileges had to be stopped for several months and the prisoners were confined to their cell blocks and compounds, while the gardens reverted to jungle.

Corruption is the easiest charge to make. It will always stick and does not have to be proved. Everywhere it is a human failing and the South Vietnamese are no exception. Moreover, it is a failing which is exacerbated by the uncertainties and anxiety of war, together with the inevitable inflation. When, added to this, there has been an enormous injection of American aid over many years, no people could have avoided corruption. Certainly corruption is widespread in South Vietnam but is, except in some cases of excessive greed common to all countries, understandable in the light of the abysmally low salaries paid by the government. For example, a Lieut.-General, apart from a car and a house, receives in pay less than $100 a month, while a private soldier gets about $25. Both would, in the United Kingdom, be entitled to supplementary social security benefits. A newspaper seller on a Saigon street corner makes two to three times what is paid to a policeman on the beat. Saigon is not exactly alone in having a police force some of whose members use their position to find ways of supplementing their income.

But corruption is relative not only to the circumstances but to the standards normally demanded of those who indulge in it. For example, when a group of Harvard professors descended on Dr. Henry Kissinger in May, 1970, after the Cambodian operation, there was in effect an implication, after the treatment accorded Mr. Dean Rusk and Mr. Walt Rostow by the academic world when they left office, that if Dr. Kissinger's answers and subsequent conduct were not satisfactory he might not be welcomed back to Harvard.[27] Any such implied threat to deny future employment is just as much bribery and corruption as offering money to influence a public official. I do not know the niceties of American law, but in English law it might have been regarded as suborning a public official in the execution of his duty, for which the maximum penalty is 10 years. The South Vietnamese have yet to learn from the American Senate the practice of undermining their government services by refusing further appointment to an official who has done his duty and carried out lawful executive orders, just because the Senate does not happen to agree with those orders, as in the case of Ambassador McMurtrie Godley on completion of his tour in Laos. Nor is petty corruption, in the 'key-money' sense, as rampant as in many African countries which excites no comment. While deploring corruption, therefore, in South Vietnam, it is an accusation which few have the right to make and which, although true, does not automatically condemn the South Vietnamese case for independence out of hand. It is only a convenient excuse for such a judgement.

If such a judgement is made on South Vietnam, it can equally be made on North Vietnam where speeches by ministers and articles in official newspapers constantly report corruption. The following brief reports are a selection for one week:

—Illegal diversion of the funds of state enterprises to purchase personal luxuries; inadequate or no receipts on more than 1·5 million piastres in expenditures by one state enterprise in Hanoi. *(Hanoi Moi,* December 12, 1973.)

—Several Hanoi enterprises illegally sell new materials as 'excess supplies', including 35 tons of wire and 3 locomotives. *(Hanoi Moi,* December 13, 1973.)

—Black market sale of clothing by students reported. *(Tien Phong,* December 13, 1973.)

—Fairly widespread and open trading of illegal grain and ration books in Hanoi; 170 tons of stolen grain recovered; 318 violations of grain regulations recorded in one month in Hanoi. *(Hanoi Moi,* December 16, 1973.)

—Black market activities in sale of bicycles, food coupons

and stolen goods; 257 persons cited by police during an inspection of only one Hanoi market area. *(Hanoi Moi,* December 18, 1973.)

Not even Saigon can rival those, but such a comparison would have been anathema to the anti-war movement, and the media ignored communist sources of information on such subjects anyway.

It is all good human stuff which only goes to show that, under communism, the people are even more inclined to pilfer from the state including items of foreign aid. There are plenty of other familiar sounding items from the same sources: illegal sale of ration coupons for purchase of cloth, sugar, rice and flour in Hanoi; excessive grain purchases by enterprises and families who exaggerate the number of members to obtain more food—thousands of cases discovered in Hanoi; truck drivers co-operate in theft of state cargoes from vans; fraudulent practice by labour contractors on construction sites—illegal commissions, skimming labourers' wages and short changing on amount of work; and favouritism in selection of trainees for foreign study. All this is obviously fair game in Hanoi, but a fraction of it would be deplorable in Saigon.

Another frequent accusation was censorship of the press. I do not think that in any other war in history, where a country has been fighting for survival, have foreign correspondents been allowed such complete freedom and facilities. South Vietnam, with all its virtues and vices, was thrown open to them; they ignored the virtues and revelled in the vices. To a certain extent the domestic Saigon press took its lead from this and most of its newspapers were critical of the GVN. There was of course censorship, but, with regard to national defence and the movement of forces, not enough. Even so 'opposition' newspapers flourished and there was at one time such open criticism of the GVN that it led Tran Ngoc Chau, then a Province Chief (but later detained for secretly dealing with his brother on the other side), to give my favourite definition of a free press: 'One that is fifty per cent for the government instead of ninety-five per cent against!'

Excluding one or two English and French and seven Chinese

newspapers, there were after 1954 eight Vietnamese news-papers in Saigon. After Diem's fall in 1963 this figure mush-roomed to 49 in 1964 but fell away to 28 by 1968. Many of these smaller papers had made their money by a system of blackmail (pay or we print). During the Thieu period the number increased again to 37 by 1972. The rise in the price of newsprint in that year caused ten of the smaller papers to close. It has always been my view that it was a mistake on the part of the GVN to have subsidized newsprint. Newspapers should have been compelled to be a practical commercial proposition. In September, 1972, in order to force a more responsible atti-tude, the GVN issued a decree requiring newspapers to make a deposit of 20 million piastres ($40,000), as a result of which five opposition and five independent newspapers closed. But one new paper appeared and another resumed publication, making a total therefore of nineteen Vietnamese newspapers — all this in a city of about two millions, although a few of the papers had a small outside circulation as well.

The total compares very favourably with Hanoi where there is one main official paper, the *Nhan Dan*, and two others (*Hanoi Moi* and *Tien Phong*) entirely under government control. It compares even more favourably with New York where there are only three morning newspapers, the leading one of which, while technically free, is limited to the publication of views which accord with those of its editorial board. In other words, it is free to publish what it likes, but not free to publish what it doesn't like.

There are many other fields of criticism which I have not covered and I accept that in all cases some fact in support could be produced. I think that, if I had only spent a short period in Vietnam confined mainly to the bars and restaurants of Saigon and the diplomatic or journalistic *milieu*, I too would have been overwhelmed by the scandals, the gossip, the inefficiency, the frustration and the crisis of the moment. On first acquaintance I had not considered the Vietnamese as attractive as other Asians I had known and, at all times, I voiced my criticism of their failings where I thought it would have the most effect. But over the years I came to recognize that these failings were very human, and indeed, inevitable in a poor country which

57

had known no peace and whose people were fighting desperately for survival as a separate state. After visiting hundreds of villages, training centres, refugee camps and paramilitary units (with which I was more concerned than with the ARVN) I learnt to appreciate the resilience of the Vietnamese, their courage, stoicism and stamina. I soon realized that their qualities and virtues far outweighed their failings and vices and now have the greatest admiration and respect for them. They surmounted national and personal crises which would have crushed most people and, in spite of casualties which would have appalled and probably collapsed the United States, they could still maintain over one million men under arms after more than ten years of war. The United Kingdom did just about that, proportionately, in 1917 after three years of war but never again. The United States has never done it.

In any case much of the criticism was maliciously exaggerated, for purposes of political profit within the United States, and most of it was irrelevant to the basic issue of the war—whether the North would take over the South by force or not. This was what really mattered to the South Vietnamese people and the question in 1969 was whether, in spite of the shortcomings and the past, the war could still be won in the sense that the North could be thwarted of its purpose and the South could be secured as a separate independent state indefinitely.

CHAPTER IV

WINNING THE UNWINNABLE

But the greatest myth, widely accepted in the United States and elsewhere, was that the war was unwinnable. Certainly it was unwinnable in the conventional sense but then this was not a conventional war. It was also unwinnable by the United States. It was winnable only by South Vietnam with American assistance. For the North, the meaning of winning was quite simple: the take-over of South Vietnam and its unification with the North under the Politburo in Hanoi—'bringing the Vietnamese people under its (the Party's) revolutionary regime'; and the establishment of satellite states in Laos and Cambodia on the principle of 'limited sovereignty'—'Asian Czechoslovakias' as Prince Sihanouk called them or, more picturesquely, 'Hanoi's private game reserve'. For the South, the meaning of winning was more difficult because it was neither so absolute nor irreversible. It was not only necessary for the South to thwart the North in its purpose but to such an extent that, whether it was renounced or not, force could not be successfully used by the North in the future so that the South would be able to maintain itself indefinitely as a separate sovereign state. (The same applied to Laos and Cambodia.) Now that was a tall order but not, with American help, impossible.

Whenever I state to an American that the war was (and still is) winnable, the immediate reaction almost without exception is that, when the United States became involved after 1965, they should have invaded and flattened the North. I can think of nothing which would have been more disastrous. Such action would not have ended the war, would have got the United States almost irretrievably embroiled in a garrison or occupying role in the whole of Indochina, might have provoked a tougher Russian or Chinese reaction, if not in Vietnam then elsewhere, and would have irreparably damaged the reputation and credibility of the United States both domestically and internationally for decades. As it was, enough damage was done in that respect by the general inclination towards a policy of employing massive military might during the period of the Johnson Administration.

The comprehensibility gap was partly caused by this failure of American military power. Few could understand how the application of such power could not achieve a victory and some felt that the answer was therefore to apply more. The confusion was compounded by the inability of the Administration itself to understand the nature of the war so that its explanations, and at times false optimism,[28] baffled the public still further. To this was added the lack of balance in reporting and the contortions of the intellectual community. This total witches' brew led to the inevitable conclusion that the war was unwinnable and, because of that, to every conceivable excuse why the war ought not to be won anyway.

I have dealt with that failure and the nature of the war in more detail in an earlier book,[29] but briefly there was an insurgency within the South initially carried out by Southerners, many of them trained in the North, but promoted, supported and directed by the Politburo in Hanoi. From 1964 onwards there was an element of invasion from the North which steadily increased as the insurgency waned until, in 1972, a conventional invasion was mounted. The insurgency and the invasion, while tactically distinguishable, were strategically inseparable as two facets of one war designed to overthrow the GVN and take over the South. That was still the position after the cease-fire with the greater emphasis on the military strength of the invading North Vietnamese Army and lesser emphasis on the insurgency, and with the Vietcong, heavily reinforced by NVA fillers, playing a minor military role and failing completely on the internal political front.

At the beginning of 1969 when President Nixon was inaugurated he had only two options: either to sell out or to continue the war. The first alternative was never seriously considered. That was made clear in his major policy speech on Vietnam on 3 November, 1969, when he said: 'The precipitate withdrawal of all American forces from Vietnam would be a disaster, not only for South Vietnam but for the United States and the cause of peace. . . . Ultimately, this would cost more lives, which would not bring peace but more war.'

In spite of the anti-war movement and the confusion within the United States this refusal to sell out was endorsed by the majority of the American people. This was later shown not only by President Nixon's overwhelming majority at his re-election in November, 1972, but also by the Gallup polls at the time when Senator McGovern announced his own sell-out policy. These showed, on the Vietnam issue alone, a majority on 13 October, 1972, in favour of the President's policy of 58 per cent to 26 per cent with 16 per cent undecided. Even in the 18–29 age group the President had a majority of 52 to 33 on this issue.

But to continue the war by following the sterile 'more of the same' strategy devised by the previous Administration was futile and not the alternative. A new long-haul low-cost strategy had to be adopted which would greatly reduce the cost both in casualties and money, thereby making it more tolerable to the American people. At the same time it had to be effective in achieving the limited aim which the President had set himself of ensuring that the people of South Vietnam would have the opportunity of determining their own future through freedom of choice and not through force. This strategy had five elements, all of which were inter-related: Vietnamization; Pacification; the containment of the invasion threat; the withdrawal of American forces; and the continuing of negotiations.

Before dealing with these in turn there are two points which must be made. By continuing the war, albeit with a new strategy, the risk had to be taken that those who never understood it and those who were maliciously inclined towards the new Administration would inevitably re-label the war as 'Nixon's war'. In fact, of course, the President was recognizing that it was entirely a South Vietnamese people's war and had to be restored to that state with the United States reverting to the role of assistance instead of being a major combatant. The second point was that the policy was never dictated by silly little considerations of face-saving. The considerations, as the President's speech of 3 November, 1969, showed, were a great deal more fundamental than that, both in relation to South Vietnam itself and to peace in the world as a whole. Those who fired such criticism merely showed a pettiness of mind which has fortunately not yet infected recent Presidents of the United States.

There were three favourable factors in South Vietnam which made the new strategy possible. While the Tet offensive in early 1968 had achieved for Hanoi a traumatic psychological victory within the United States, it was a military disaster for its promoters within South Vietnam. The attempt to repeat it in May and again in August of 1968 (which hardly got off the ground) merely increased the disaster. The offensive cost Hanoi, and especially the Vietcong, the cream of their regular forces and the tactics were suicidal to the junior leadership. Even General Giap at the end of 1969 admitted to total casualties—killed, deserted and seriously wounded—during the previous two years of more than half a million men. That would have been equivalent in the United States to losing an army of about five million men or in the United Kingdom to a failure to rescue a single man from three Dunkirks. As subsequent events showed, the Vietcong were broken as a military threat and the North Vietnamese Army did not recover for two years. Secondly, although severely but only temporarily shaken at the time, the people of South Vietnam were galvanized by the offensive which really brought the war into the towns for the first time. The atrocities committed at Hue and elsewhere removed the velvet glove from the iron hand and, far from engineering any form of spontaneous uprisings in support, produced a counter-reaction which resulted in the complete mobilization of the South Vietnamese people against the invader. It was at this point that the South Vietnamese people began to identify their enemy as being the North Vietnamese Army and not the Vietcong. Finally, and I amongst others did not immediately recognize this point, the concentration of the forces of both sides on the towns had left a vacuum in the rural areas. The side which recovered first would gain a rich reward. It was this vacuum which made the accelerated pacification programme both safe and timely.

Of all the five elements in the new strategy Vietnamization was the most important. It was most frequently represented as

'turning the war over to the Vietnamese' and there were some
who thought that the United States could almost in one
moment of time stand aside and let the Vietnamese get on
with it, whereas the real point was to improve Vietnamese
performance in all fields. Owing to the neglect of this policy
during the previous years while the war was fought as an
American war, there was much constructive work required
which would take several years. As Mr. Melvin Laird, the
American Secretary of Defense who was entrusted with the
policy, declared; Vietnamization required 'a stronger Administration, a stronger economy, stronger military forces and
stronger police for internal security'. All those go together and
stronger military forces alone would not be enough, although
quite rightly they were the first priority. The Tet offensive had
revealed that the NVA and the Vietcong, with their new
Russian weapons including the AK 47 rifle, were better
armed and had a higher fire power on the ground than the
South Vietnamese forces. The re-equipment of ARVN, including the issue of M 16 rifles right down to the Popular
Forces defending the villages, quickly redressed this balance.
At the same time the size of the forces was greatly increased
from about 600,000 to over 1 million, with the main emphasis
on the Regional Forces (fighting in their own provinces) and
the Popular Forces (defending their own villages). The programmes for the Navy and Air Force were accelerated. It
would be pointless, and boring, to go into detail on all these.
They are on the record.

There was, however, one major weakness in both equipment
and the structure of the forces. The whole design was defensive.
There was no question at any time of equipping the South
Vietnamese Army with weapons which might have enabled it
to attack North Vietnamese supply routes and rear bases or
even to conduct an effective counter-offensive. It was not even
equipped to withstand a major conventional invasion. The
structure of the forces, already defensive, was based on the
concept of defending territory, especially populated territory,
throughout the country. This meant that there was little flexibility in the deployment of forces because nearly all of them
were already allocated to the defence of a particular area,

with the army divided into four Regions and with only two divisions (the Airborne and the Marines) in national reserve. It was even more inflexible at the lower levels where Regional Forces were confined to their own province and Popular Force platoons to their own villages. It took a lot of time and effort to achieve more flexibility in moving forces across these arbitrary boundaries. Finally, there were still problems in the command structure—not at the top where President Thieu was firmly in control of his generals—but, for example, when Naval and Air Force units were allocated to Regions the question arose, how far did they come under the command of the Army Regional Commander or stay under command of their headquarters in Saigon. At a lower level there were still problems with regard to the operational control of ARVN battalions or regiments allocated to a province to support pacification. But these problems of command and co-ordination had always been there and are common in all countries. They were much nearer to a solution in Vietnam in the 1970s than they were in the 1960s.

No immediate progress was made in respect of the National Police Force. Its main weakness stemmed from its being the Cinderella of all the forces. It was not even allowed to recruit anyone between the ages of 18 and 37. The force as a whole had no standing in the community and few members of the Force had career status. More than three-quarters were on a 'daily paid' basis. The great majority operated out of headquarters in the major province and district towns. Not until late in 1971 was a real start made on rectifying these deficiencies. Limited recruiting was opened for career policemen at the age of 18, including officers. Police officers were given equivalent army rank and status. The command structure was improved, but above all the Force was deployed down to a lower level. Stations were opened in all villages and towns and became, as they should be, the basic operating unit of the Force providing the policeman on the beat in contact with his own community, thus enabling the Police Force to play a fuller part both in internal security and in maintaining law and order. It was remarkable that during the whole of this period there was hardly a terrorist incident in Saigon and I can say with complete personal conviction that Saigon was a safer place in which to live and walk around both by day and night than most American cities.

I have always been a strong advocate of the importance of the administrative structure in defeating an insurgency—and for that matter an invasion—because at all times a government must function. It was perhaps the greatest advantage that Malaya during its Emergency had over Vietnam that government policies could be fairly and effectively implemented through the administrative departments. Throughout the 1960s Saigon had built up some top-heavy ministries and thousands of ill-trained 'cadres', who could provide few practical benefits for the villages. Most benefits came from American aid, from the building of schools down to the distribution of pigs. The weakness was partly due to the fact that few Americans had been prepared to take a long-term view and were impatient for quick results. Whereas a soldier can be trained in a few months, it takes years to produce doctors or civil engineers and, at the next level, nurses and public works foremen. The rebuilding of the administration, therefore, down to village level needed time and, to save it, some demobilization of trained manpower from the forces. But it is worth recording what an English journalist, visiting South Vietnam in 1973 after an absence of many years, had to say on this point: 'Who would have thought, amongst the panic, graft and intrigue that passed for administration then, that South Vietnam would acquire a tolerably functional civil service? Saigon's government offices may still be far from Westminster's standards of dedication and efficiency, but at least nowadays they seem to work.'[30]

The re-organization, improvement and expansion of the GVN's whole military and civil structure with the aim of achieving better performance depended on both the willingness of the people to support it politically and of the country being able to support it economically. I have already dealt with the political support expressed through the electoral system, but the real evidence lies in the fact that, in a population of 19 millions of whom more than half were under 18 years of age, the country was able to raise and maintain forces over 1 million strong. Certainly there was conscription to compel recruitment but there was no problem in obtaining recruits for the élite units in ARVN or for the territorial forces, except in some provinces where the population was sparse and the need often greatest, because it was in these areas that the old traditional Vietcong bases lay. In comparison the Vietcong within the South had the greatest difficulty in recruitment and in the years after 1969 their units were more and more filled by NVA soldiers. There was, however, in the South Vietnamese forces a high rate of draft dodgers and deserters, often seasonal because of planting and harvesting, but cases of defection to the Vietcong were very rare. Lieutenant-General Hoang Xuan Lam, who commanded Military Region I for many years, once said to me: 'If six Popular Force platoons (150 men) defect with their arms to the enemy, I will ring up President Thieu and tell him that we have lost the war.' That telephone call has never been made.

In many ways this was remarkable because the South Vietnamese armed forces were constantly subjected to subtle and intensive psychological warfare by the other side, who were of the same race and masters of the art. At the same time ARVN's fighting qualities and performance were denigrated by their ally to an extent which would have demoralized most armies. What is more, right through the war, they took heavy casualties. Even between 1965 and 1968 South Vietnamese killed in action exceeded American casualties in every week except three. By 1969 they were running at three to four times the American rate and this ratio steadily increased as American forces were withdrawn from the country or at least from combat. There were none of the compelling sanctions which a communist system can apply, such as execution and loss of rights for the family.

No one could expect an agricultural country in this wartime situation to be able to support such forces financially without outside help, quite apart from military equipment. There was no hope of the revenue meeting the salaries bill however low the salaries were. The import programme was bound to exceed any possible exports twenty times over. Even with improved security, greater prosperity and heavier taxation, the gap between revenue and expenditure was still enormous and could only be met by American aid. Every effort was however made to increase taxation and improve its collection, although naturally unpopular. I remember discussing taxation with the Economics Minister and we got on to import duties which are, after all, the easiest to impose and collect. He mentioned that in many instances a straight import duty could be avoided by the rich and fell on the poor. He quoted the car as an example where the import duty was very high but, when the rich sold a car after a year or so, most of the tax was passed on down the line and fell disproportionately on the last owner who drove the car until it was wrecked. He was, therefore, proposing to change this tax to an annual tax based on the licence so that the greatest proportion was paid in the first and second years and therefore fell on the rich who bought the new car. There are not many Ministers who look at their taxation problems in this way.

But the next priority in 1969 was to get the economy moving again. I can remember flying over the Mekong Delta just after the Tet offensive and seeing not a single truck, other than military convoys, moving on the roads nor boats on any of the canals. In 1969 this changed completely as roads, bridges and canals were repaired and opened. The figures speak for themselves. The rice harvest went up from 5,115,000 metric tons in 1969 to 6,324,000 in 1971 and the area under cultivation from 1,780,000 hectares* in 1969 to over 2,000,000 at the beginning of 1972. Rubber output also recovered slightly from 27,650 metric tons in 1969 to 37,500 in 1971. New strains of rice, such as IR 8, were introduced thereby increasing the yield and also enabling, in some areas, two or even three crops to be grown annually. The surplus of rice was reflected in a greatly increased output of pigs, ducks and chickens for which cereals could now be spared by the producing farmers. In areas close to towns and markets vegetable production increased enormously, and some rice fields were entirely diverted to such crops. The increased prosperity has frequently been referred to as 'the Honda boom'. Certainly Hondas, television sets and

* One hectare = 2·47 acres.

transistors announced the arrival of the consumer society in South Vietnam's farming community. But there was also considerable investment in water pumps for improved irrigation, in outboard motors for sampans and fishing vessels and, above all, in tractors. By the end of 1971 there were nearly 40,000 tractors in South Vietnam, of which more than 12,000 were over 30 horse power. They were not gifts, but were bought and owned by individual farmers or co-operatives. Because of the stagnant 1930s, the Japanese occupation and the first Indochina war the Vietnamese farmer had been completely left behind in the modernization process. This was the 'revolution' required and it was achieved even in war through the incentive of free enterprise. All this increased production enabled South Vietnam to become almost self-supporting in food by the end of 1971 and to slow down the spiral of inflation. Prosperity was giving the farmer a greater stake not only in the security of his own area but in the defence of the country as a whole.

While I have included the economic revival under Vietnamization, the programmes which helped to achieve it were mostly carried out through the second element in the new strategy under the heading of Pacification. Pacification in Vietnam, from the poorly directed and inefficiently implemented strategic hamlet programme through new life hamlets and revolutionary development, had had an ill-fated history. Americans tended to shy off it for one simple reason; it was bound to take time. When a government has been pushed back by the insurgent strategy known as 'using the villages to encircle the towns', so that large areas of the countryside are under insurgent control while other areas are contested, the reversal of this process is likely to take almost as long as it has taken the insurgent to gain territorial control. By 1965, therefore, it could have been said that, after six years of Vietcong expansion, it would take the government at least five years to reverse it. This was too long for the United States. Pacification, therefore, was given a low priority and all the emphasis was placed on military operations against the NVA and Vietcong military units. Few realized that it was the main task of these units to keep American and Vietnamese forces away from pacification. By 1968 the time which pacification might have been expected to take had been even further extended. If I had been asked at that time how long pacification would take, I would probably have replied eight to ten years. But that time factor was entirely altered by the Tet offensive because not only Vietcong regular units but the best of their regional forces, which would normally have defended their areas against pacification, were lost in the attack on the towns. This provided the opportunity, and fortunately the GVN was in a position to take it.

For the first time, as a result of the re-organization of the American and Vietnamese military and civil departments concerned, a comprehensive and co-ordinated plan for 1969 had been produced. Moreover, pacification now received the priority it deserved. Because of the vacuum in the countryside already mentioned, the results in the first year were quite spectacular and the plan was fulfilled by the end of October. The targets required that by that date over 50 per cent of the hamlets in the country should be classified as 'A' or 'B', that is under government control with a high degree of security, and a further 40 per cent as 'C', that is under government control with a lesser degree of security. No one would have believed it possible a year before and the high points of military activity initiated by the NVA during the dry season of 1969 did nothing to stop it. During 1970 and 1971 the criteria for 'A' and 'B' hamlets were constantly raised but nevertheless by March, 1972, 70 per cent of the hamlets were 'A' or 'B' which, with the towns, contained over 80 per cent of the population. At this time only 2 per cent of the hamlets (226) were classified as Vietcong, with less than 1 per cent of the population. This was not achieved by pulling people back into secure areas. On the contrary, they were encouraged to return to their villages in areas which had previously been held by the Vietcong.

Territory was regained by weight of numbers. It was not just the expanded Regional Forces and Popular Forces going back and securing hamlets and villages which had been under Vietcong control; it was also the people going with them and those still in the area welcoming them. These last included Vietcong rank and file, who in 1969 were rallying to the government at the rate of 4,000 a month. This figure naturally declined over the next two years, but even in 1971 it was averaging 1,800 a month. In the celebrated province of Kien Hoa, many areas of which had been under Vietcong control from early Vietminh days at the end of World War II, it was fascinating to visit villages where the Popular Forces defending them were composed entirely of ex-Vietcong. On 2 September, 1970, Bui Cong Tuong, the leading Vietcong responsible for guerrillas in Kien Hoa surrendered. His reason for doing so was that at one time he had had about 10,000 armed guerrillas under his command. When this figure dropped to 3,000 he decided that the government was winning. He was not alone in his view. The people understood it too, with the result that the whole balance of manpower and resources shifted radically in the government's favour. This meant that the Vietcong, including NVA units then inside South Vietnam, were being confined to their traditional base areas such as the U Minh forest and Camau Peninsula in the south, the Plain of Reeds on the Cambodian border round the Parrot's Beak, Zone C and the Saigon river corridor (again on the Cambodian border north and east of Tay Ninh), and the central mountain chain mainly opposite the coastal provinces between Danang and Qui Nhon.

There was one exception which came to be known as 'the mini bases'. These were corridors for movement, particularly along creeks, and small base areas of scrub and swamp close to populated areas whose retention was essential if the Vietcong were to maintain any threat at all to the population. The mini bases could not be held by Vietcong units in any strength because they would have immediately been engaged and destroyed. They were held instead by very small elusive squads using the most concentrated system of booby traps which have ever been laid, thereby making it impossible for government forces to enter such areas without suffering heavy casualties at no corresponding expense to the Vietcong. All through 1970 and 1971 much time and effort was devoted to the slow gradual clearance of these mini bases. For example, in Dinh Tuong province, about 60 miles south of Saigon, thousands of territorial forces were employed on this task between 2 November and 10 December, 1971, and out of 320 casualties 290 were from booby traps.

A point to be made here is that pacification is not completed merely by clearing the insurgent out of the developed populated areas. He must also be denied access to, and freedom of movement in, the neighbouring uninhabited areas. This is not just a matter of local territorial force patrols being able to enter such areas at will but of the people themselves, who are the eyes and ears of their own local forces, being able to enter these areas for legitimate purposes such as woodcutting and fishing, or even to extend their cultivated areas. It is people going about their ordinary everyday life, as much as forces, which helps to keep insurgents out at a time when events are moving in favour of the government. A very good example of this is the interdiction of roads. When the tide is moving in favour of the insurgent then the blowing of a bridge or the cutting of a road will automatically stop all traffic. People get the message and are warned off by it. When, however, the tide is moving in the government's favour then such incidents have little effect on traffic. A way is immediately found round any obstruction until it is repaired and traffic goes on. It is this determination not to be put off by minor incidents which is one of the clear indicators of a successful pacification programme.

Even by October, 1969, when I was first invited by President Nixon to go out to Vietnam and to let him have a first hand, candid and independent report on the situation, I was most impressed by this aspect of security. Not only was I able to visit areas and walk through villages which had been under Vietcong control for years, but I had never felt so relaxed when travelling round the country. Taking into account the success of the pacification programme, the increased security, the improving economy and the complete change in the relative strength and capability of the opposing forces, I was able to report to the President on 3 December, as he announced in a broadcast on 15 December, in the following cautiously optimistic terms:

'I was very impressed by the improvement in the military and political situation in Vietnam as compared with all previous visits, and especially in the security situation, both in Saigon and the rural areas. A winning position, in the sense of obtaining a just peace, whether negotiated or not, and of maintaining an independent non-communist South Vietnam has been achieved, but we are not yet through.'

The complaint levelled at pacification and counter-insurgency by such critics as the 'concerned Asian scholars', that its whole concept was designed to restore the status quo, bore no relation to what was happening during this period. In fact, their criticism was based on an interpretation of earlier years and it is hard to believe that any of them has ever visited a country where an insurgency has been successfully countered. The social and political changes which occurred during the Emergency in Malaya were radical and, fortunately, not revolutionary in the violent sense. The same can be said of South Vietnam. Indeed many of the programmes covered by such loose terms as pacification are designed to produce exactly that effect. Just one example of these in South Vietnam was the 'land to the tiller' programme. The land reform initiated by President Diem had already reduced rice land ownership to units of 100 hectares or less. This was now carried further and, by the end of September, 1973, 934,111 hectares of land had been distributed to 605,515 new owners who received titles to their holdings, with a further 201,615 hectares in the process of being distributed to 128,103 people (on the average about $3\frac{1}{2}$ acres each).

Some social effects of material prosperity are perhaps regrettable. The change from a subsistence economy under which villages were self-contained and self-reliant to a market economy has meant that the villages and village families have become less directly responsible for their own social problems: for example, in providing for aged and sick relatives, widows and orphans. This problem is now beginning to fall on the state. The mechanization of agriculture, improved education and the attraction of wage-earning employment are also partly responsible for the move of population from the villages to the towns. This inevitable process was accelerated by the war.

The political changes were also radical as a result of national and provincial elections, and the villages themselves were administered by an elected village council. A false report was

disseminated in the United States in 1972 that President Thieu
had abolished such local elections. Under new decrees promul-
gated in that year the election of hamlet chiefs only was abolished,
but elected Village Councils including elected village chiefs
remained. The new decree also reduced the size of Village
Councils to the more manageable number of eight members
for villages over 5,000 and six members for under 5,000. Each
Village Council continued to administer an average of 4–5
hamlets in its area. I have always maintained that, except in
rare large ones, the hamlet never could be a viable administrative unit and that all local authority at the lowest level should
be centred in the Village Council and the village chief. But the
real political change was that Nguyen Van Thieu, the son of a
village chief in a rural area of central Vietnam about 150 miles
north of Saigon, could rise to the Presidency.

While Vietnamization and Pacification were the priority
programmes from 1969 onwards, this did not mean that the
major military effort could be diverted from the need to contain the invasion element of the war. Although, under General
Creighton Abrams, the military policy was changed from
'search and destroy' to 'clear and hold', a major effort still had
to be devoted, as part of 'hold', to keeping regular NVA units
out of the populated areas. This was the chief task of the remaining United States forces, but it was increasingly being
taken over by ARVN.

In considering the defence of South Vietnam against the
invasion element of the threat, the most significant but seldom
mentioned point is the geographical shape of South Vietnam
itself. It is a long narrow country of about 700 miles from the
DMZ to the tip of the Camau Peninsula and little more than
100 miles wide, and in many places much less. If it had been
surrounded by sea, except on the DMZ (as in South Korea),
there would have been no problem at all; the war would have
been won years ago and the North could have been held at bay
indefinitely. If it had been square or round it would still have
been much easier to defend, with internal lines of communication allowing forces to be more compact and concentrated and
to be quickly deployed to a critical point. Under the Vietnamization programme, for example, a much smaller air force

would have been needed because operations on any front could have been supported from one central group of air fields instead of four.

But unfortunately these geographical advantages did not exist. The western border from the DMZ in the north to Ha Tien in the south runs for over 600 miles, excluding indentations, with the northern section of 400 miles bordering on Laos and north-east Cambodia in hilly almost unpopulated jungle, and the last 200 miles through comparatively flat country composed mainly of scrub and swamp, and, in the more populated areas beside the Mekong river, rice fields. It has no natural defensive features and, against an enemy who has complete freedom of movement and action within Laos and Cambodia, is almost militarily indefensible because such an enemy can build up his forces without interruption and can attack at a point and time of his own choosing. Owing to the narrowness of South Vietnam such attacks, given any initial momentum, must penetrate into the heart of the country. The South Vietnamese, on the other hand, in defence have to cover the whole length of the frontier and therefore to spread their forces thinly all down the country. This meant that the enemy could always achieve a superiority of numbers at his chosen point and so engage and maul inferior forces before forces from other areas could be moved in as reinforcements. In all the arguments about the fighting quality of the South Vietnamese soldier, it has to be remembered that, in nearly every action fought, the numerical superiority of the NVA was locally greater. They would not have attacked if that had not been the case.

At the beginning of 1969 the North Vietnamese Army was in full control of considerable areas of southern Laos (in violation of the 1962 Geneva Agreement on Laos) through which ran the Ho Chi Minh trail. They also occupied, and had sanctuaries secure against eviction in, north-eastern Cambodia as far south as the Parrot's Beak opposite Saigon, with up to four divisions in that supposedly neutral country. While their forces in Laos and northern Cambodia, down to about the 12th Parallel opposite Nha Trang, were supplied down the trail, those south of that line were supplied through Sihanoukville (now Kampong Som) by Russian and Chinese ships. The estimated tonnage of military supplies and equipment which came through this port up to 1970 was 25,000 tons. This, of course, excluded rice which was readily available in Cambodia. Not even with South Vietnamese forces increased to over a million and the presence of over half a million American troops in the country could NVA incursions across this border be prevented. In spite of the military failure of the Tet offensive, the North Vietnamese retained the same army unit structure, thereby showing that their intention of maintaining the invasion element of the threat had not changed. There was, however, a fall in the infiltration rate down the Ho Chi Minh trail in 1969 as compared with the exceptional numbers which had been poured in during 1968. This decrease was caused partly by floods in North Vietnam and by monsoon conditions along the trail, which were made worse through American bombing with the approval of the Royal Lao Government. As a further indication of intentions, several NVA units were moved further south within Cambodia in order to infiltrate into the lower part of the Mekong Delta. These included the NVA 1st Division, some of which eventually ended up in the U Minh forest. One of its regiments was 95A, which had been the first major unit to enter South Vietnam in October, 1964, in the area of Kontum.

Through 1969 there were a number of high points, but because of NVA units still being much under-strength there was no sustained offensive. A further reason for this was the weakness of the Vietcong strength in the countryside, which made it difficult for forward supplies to be pre-positioned for NVA units crossing the border. One feature of the Tet offensive had been that whole NVA divisions had been able to maintain themselves for weeks on end, even close to Saigon, because of well-prepared dumps and caches of food and ammunition. The new 'clear and hold' strategy, particularly in key areas on the lines of incursion, prevented the Vietcong from stocking food and ammunition in advance, with the result that NVA units could not maintain themselves operationally within South Vietnam for any length of time.

With the withdrawal of US forces beginning in 1969 the threat from the borders was obviously going to become more acute. To take an English soccer analogy, it was as if the NVA from its sanctuaries in Laos and Cambodia was being given a free penalty shot at goal along a 600-mile wide goal mouth. The obvious answer in those circumstances was to take the ball further back up the field away from the goal mouth. The opportunity for this was provided by the revolt in Cambodia against the presence of NVA divisions on Cambodian soil. This revolt occurred in the spring of 1970 under Marshal Lon Nol and had the support at that time of all leading Cambodian politicians and all sections of the population, other than certain elements of the Khmer Rouge who supported the North Vietnamese and who were opposed to any government in Phnom Penh including that of Prince Sihanouk. The latter was out of the country at the time on a visit to Moscow, and there was some speculation that he too, as the unwilling host, had become disenchanted with his guests who had been breaching Cambodian neutrality for several years. He may well have been seeking Russian help to restrain them. But the Russians rapidly washed their hands of this problem and of the Prince, who was passed on to the Chinese.

The Cambodian operation, ably conducted by Lieut.-General Mike Davison then commanding the American Second Field Force, and including South Vietnamese divisions from Regions III and IV under their own command, was unfortunately limited both in time and space and was directed mainly at the sanctuaries and supply dumps built up by the North Vietnamese close to the border. Nevertheless, quite apart from the supplies destroyed, the operation had three important strategic results. It prevented the North Vietnamese from immediately over-running Cambodia and saved Phnom Penh, thereby giving the new government time to build up the Cambodian Army which was only 28,000 strong, ill-equipped, and untrained. But, far more important, it closed Sihanoukville as an NVA supply port. This meant that in the future all supplies for NVA forces in Cambodia and for the Vietcong in the southern portion of South Vietnam would have to be re-routed down the Ho Chi Minh trail, and that the organization on the trail would have to be greatly expanded to cope with the traffic. There were some doubts within the

United States as to how much time the Cambodian operation had gained in this respect. My own view, expressed at the time to Dr. Kissinger, was that it had gained at least a year, probably eighteen months and possibly two years, before the North Vietnamese would be in any position to conduct serious operations again below about the 12th Parallel. As the third strategic result it showed that President Nixon was prepared to take positive action with American forces, both as a means of safeguarding the remaining American forces in South Vietnam and in support of his whole Vietnamization policy.

This last had its effect also in other theatres. There was at that time in 1970 a grave danger that the Middle East situation would erupt again. Israel was requesting the immediate delivery of fifty more Phantoms from the United States. I happened to lunch with the Israeli Minister from their Embassy in London when the Cambodian operations started and my opening remark to him was: 'That's worth more than a squadron of Phantoms to you, isn't it?' He agreed that, from the point of view of Israel's adversaries, it had made the response of the US Sixth Fleet in the Mediterranean unpredictable. There was no renewal of the Middle East war in that year. But, while the operation was a stabilizing factor outside the United States, it had exactly the opposite effect within the States, leading to violent anti-war demonstrations which culminated in the shooting of four students by the National Guard at Kent State University. It led to some comment that American foreign policy would no longer be formed by the Administration but would be made in the streets.

It is not the purpose of this book to chart the course of dissent within the United States, but obviously, because of its effect on American will, the pressure generated by it was, as we shall see, a major factor to be taken into account in all subsequent decisions. Such decisions could not therefore always be taken on the strict merits of the war situation at the time and had to be modified or tuned to mollify the dissenters. For example, troop withdrawals could never be presented as a reduction of forces because of the improving situation. They had to be presented solely as getting out. By undermining American credibility dissent became one of the reasons why a real peace in Vietnam could not be achieved and why there is now such a dangerous situation facing the United States.

When I paid another visit to South Vietnam in October, 1970, it was quite clear that continued progress had been made in both the Pacification and Vietnamization programmes during the year, so that the 1969 gains were expanded and consolidated. With over 90 per cent of the populated countryside under GVN control, and over one million men under arms, future progress in these two programmes would inevitably be less spectacular. Progress was most visible in the expanding secure rural road networks and in the increased traffic on both roads and canals. In 1969 the two major programmes while going well had still been fragile. Although in 1970 they were not yet completed and were still an enemy target, they had reached a point where they were unassailable and could no longer be interrupted or reversed by the Vietcong or by NVA incursions. In military capability, manpower and territorial security the GVN was immeasurably stronger and the enemy much weaker. One of my most pleasant experiences was to drive round villages in Quang Tin province completely unescorted on the back of the District Chief's Honda, in an area where, two years before, the district town itself had been invested and only just held. We were greeted with friendly smiles and cups of tea but it was noticeable that, in every house, there was a weapon lying handy for village defence.

The main reason for the improved situation, apart from the success of the two programmes themselves, was the destruction of the enemy's bases and stocks in Cambodia and the loss of Sihanoukville as a port of supply. His manpower losses, the problem of extending his supply trails from Laos into northeast Cambodia and the commitment of his under-strength units in Cambodia had reduced the NVA military threat in Regions III and IV to negligible proportions for at least the next year and this period could be extended by ARVN spoiling operations during the following dry season.

This situation enabled the fourth element in the new strategy — the withdrawal of US forces — to continue as planned. I had first discussed withdrawal of forces with Dr. Kissinger in October, 1968, while he was still foreign affairs adviser to

Governor Nelson Rockefeller and before President Nixon was elected. I had suggested that, if the strategy was changed, it should be possible in the first year to reduce the forces by 100,000 (from 542,000) and to halve the cost of the war (from about 30 billion dollars annually). There were not many who would have believed this possible at the time without a collapse in South Vietnam. The first withdrawal of 25,000 men was announced in June, 1969, when President Nixon met President Thieu at Guam and enunciated the Nixon Doctrine. Within two years, by the summer of 1971, the total forces had been halved and by the beginning of 1972 they were down to under 100,000 men with only three combat infantry battalions left in the country for the defence of American installations. It was these continuing withdrawals and the prospect of abolishing the draft, at least for men going to Vietnam, which took the steam out of the anti-war movement in the United States after 1970.

From the very beginning of his Administration, President Nixon was under great pressure to withdraw all American forces. Personalities such as Mr. Clark Clifford, the former Secretary of Defense, were stating that American forces could be reduced to 200,000 in a support and logistic role by the end of 1970, without any regard for the situation in South Vietnam or for the need to retain balanced forces during the initial phase of the withdrawals for their own defence. When the figure of 200,000 was reached in the late summer of 1971, very few appreciated that the remaining forces were almost completely dependent on ARVN for their protection from that point onwards until the ceasefire. Some earlier supporters of the war, whether from a change of judgement or failure of nerve, demanded immediate and precipitate withdrawal, while others like them, including many Senators, demanded a fixed target date often less than twelve months ahead. There was little to choose between them. The first were deserters and the second were deadliners, who were really no more than deserters lacking even the courage to desert. With the number of Americans killed in action over ten years approaching 50,000 and with the enormous sums expended, they both argued: 'Surely we have done enough?' That is not a question that should ever be put by any Christian, parent, friend or ally.

The British did not put it to the French after suffering 60,000 casualties (19,000 killed) *in one day* on the Somme in 1916 to relieve the pressure on Verdun. Perhaps they should have put it to the Americans in 1942. The question did not come well from a country which a few years before had been exhorted to 'pay any price'. It augurs ill for the future, too, coming as it does from a people who have not yet been tested by major sacrifices.

This had its effect on the fifth element in the President's strategy — the continuation of negotiations, with which I deal in greater detail in Chapter VII. While the deserters and dead-liners remained vocal there was no pressure on Hanoi to nego-tiate or to make any concession which might have produced a settlement. This led to a situation where, instead, increasing pressure developed on the President to make all the concessions because of a natural aspiration for 'peace', enhanced by an even greater desire to secure the release of American POWs. Here, as we shall see, was to be the weak point in the whole strategy. Hanoi saw it too, and later exploited it to the full.

Although under pressure to desert his ally and leave the South Vietnamese to their fate, irrespective of the consequences, the President resisted the temptation to lose his predecessor's unpopular war and stood firm. In fact, after the announcement of the first withdrawal in the summer of 1969, further with-drawals were temporarily postponed as a result of the NVA's high points and it was laid down that they would depend on three criteria: the increased capability of the South Vietnamese forces, progress in the peace talks, and a lowering of activity by Hanoi and the NLF. The President did not even use the opportunity of his courageous speech on 3 November, 1969, outlining his Vietnam policy, to announce future withdrawals.

However, the strength of the anti-war movement, the general disillusion and the consequential loss of American will made it impolitic to present the withdrawals as troop reductions made possible by a steadily improving situation. Instead it was accepted that the United States were getting out from an un-popular war and turning it over to the Vietnamese. This view led to the belief, which is having great repercussions in South East Asia and elsewhere, that the United States were withdrawing from further commitments in addition to Indochina, and also helped to confirm the comforting myth that the war was unwinnable anyway. This last robbed the President of much support which might otherwise have stayed with him. The very fact that 450,000 American troops had been withdrawn by the beginning of 1972 without the place falling apart caused little comment and did not register. It would have been regarded as unbelievable and impossible in 1968 by members of the previous Administration and the whole of Congress. It was also inconceivable that, when 'the best and the brightest' had dismally failed, a Republican Administration under President Nixon was succeeding. To all his political opponents winning the war was unforgivable. It had Hanoi, and the Russians, worried too.

CHAPTER V

HANOI'S VIEWPOINT

The Politburo of the Indochina Communist Party (now more commonly known as the Lao Dong or Workers' Party) in Hanoi in 1970 was composed of six men: Le Duan, First Secretary of the Party and a former head of the Central Office for South Vietnam (COSVN); Truong Chinh, Chairman of the Standing Committee of the National Assembly and historian of the Party; Pham Von Dong, Prime Minister; Pham Hung, Member of the Secretariat and head of COSVN from 1967 to at least August, 1972; Vo Nguyen Giap, Minister of Defence and Chairman of the Central Military Party Committee; and Le Duc Tho, a member of the Secretariat responsible for organization (and for negotiations) and also a former head of COSVN. They were all original members of the Indochina Communist Party which, as a party, is strictly orthodox and Stalinist in its outlook. For example, it supported the Russian invasions of Hungary and Czechoslovakia. After a long struggle these six have been in power for twenty years, which is almost unique in the world today. They are all well over 60, and some of them have been in jail for long periods. For example, Le Duc Tho spent eleven years in jail during French rule. They represent, even in a communist context, the most reactionary regime in the world today, and one that is certainly quite unchangeable except by internal purge or mortality.

The death of Ho Chi Minh in 1969 in no way affected their policy or intentions. In fact the testament of Ho Chi Minh has merely reinforced them. It is worth noting that Ho Chi Minh himself was a member and chief agent of the Communist International in the Far East in the 1920s. He was also a founder member of the French Communist Party. He himself did not return to Vietnam until the end of World War II, after having been absent for over thirty years. The fact that he was immediately able to take over the leadership of the Indochina Communist Party at that point is significant. It resulted from his standing in the Communist International, which implied

Russian support, and his apparent backing by the Office of Strategic Services (OSS), the predecessor of the CIA, which implied American support. Both of these seemed vital to the party in its coming struggle, not only with the French but with its rival Vietnamese nationalist parties.

There has been, and still is, only one real threat to the Politburo and the Indochina Communist Party; and that, of course, is a non-communist Vietnamese nationalist party or parties. It is for this reason that the North cannot tolerate a separate successful South Vietnam, offering greater political and personal liberty and a more prosperous economy. It was the comparative success of President Diem in these respects, after 1954, which made the second Indochina war inevitable. But an overt invasion on the North Korean model at that time was out of the question because of lack of capability, because of the effect which it would have had on international opinion, and of the likely response of the United States. The alternative instrument was, however, to hand in the old Vietminh organization, which had remained in the South after 1954, and in the military guerrillas of southern birth, estimated at about 80,000, who had been repatriated to the North after the Geneva Agreements. The former was revitalized by Le Duan himself, who was specially sent to the South for that purpose, and subsequently became known as the Vietcong, while the re-infiltration into the South of the latter in the early 1960s gave the whole movement added impulse. When the 80,000 southerners ran out, NVA reinforcements were then infiltrated into the South, as confirmed by the ICC report of 2 June, 1962.[31] To cloak its direct involvement the Politburo established in 1960 the National Liberation Front but, throughout the war, itself retained overall control of all activities within the South. Even after the ceasefire in 1973 it was the Deputy Chief of Staff of the North Vietnamese Army, General Tran Van Tra, himself a southerner by birth, who appeared as the head of the Vietcong delegation to the Four Party Joint Military Commission.

Although much has been written about the war up to the period with which we are concerned from 1969 onwards, there were two interesting decisions taken by Hanoi which have not received much attention. After the fall of President Diem and during the following disastrous year of 1964, it was quite clear that the Vietcong within the South were militarily winning. Why then in October, 1964, did the North Vietnamese begin the infiltration of regular North Vietnamese military units? The decision must have been taken early in 1964, if not late in 1963 soon after the fall of President Diem. It was certainly taken before the Tonkin Gulf incident and well before there was any question of committing American combat troops, because the units must have been prepared, trained and moving during the summer of 1964. 95A Regiment entered the Central Highlands through Kontum province in October, and carried out its first action in that month on Route 19 between Qui Nhon and Pleiku. Certainly the decision may have been made in order to exploit the disarray after the fall of Diem and to accelerate the fall of the South. But, the fall of the South to what? If the NLF and the Vietcong alone were successful there was always the risk that, although communist, they might harbour some of the separatist nationalist views of the South and become averse to a Northern takeover. If, however, the North at the time of the expected victory in 1965 had its units well placed inside the South, then unification could be assured.

The second decision was that of putting Vietcong units, both regular battalions and provincial forces, into the forefront of the battle in the towns during the Tet offensive, with NVA divisions playing a less conspicuous role on the outskirts. It could be argued that, if a popular uprising was to be engineered, it was the Vietcong who should do it. But, to what extent did the Politburo really believe that the population would rise? Was their intelligence that bad? Anyway, the effect of the decision was to destroy the Vietcong as a military force. From that point onwards the military brunt of the war had to be borne by the NVA, which was certainly fighting for unification. It was now their war—a point which was not lost on the South Vietnamese.

In spite of its losses during 1968 the North Vietnamese Army did not alter its offensive posture or the structure of its forces in Laos or Cambodia. All units, however low their manpower or morale, were maintained and there were no amalgamations. Hanoi's intention obviously was to rebuild them with reinforcements from the North. Although, as we have seen in the previous chapter, high points (or high tides as the communists called them) were attempted in 1969 at Tet, and later on the normal incursion routes, these all failed. Again in 1970, after a high reinforcement rate beginning in late 1969, further offensives were planned but these were forestalled by the Cambodian operation. There were plenty of minor battles, but mainly against frontier posts a long way from any major centres of population. These merely engaged a few ARVN units, cost the North Vietnamese more casualties and made little impression within the South. The point was that this pattern of NVA raiding operations along the frontiers could only have effect if it was complementary to Vietcong operations within the populated areas of the South. In other words, the two elements of the war, invasion and revolutionary war had to work together.

This was well understood by the North and resulted in the well-known COSVN Directive No. 9, which emphasized the need to rebuild the Vietcong apparatus in the South, especially in the villages. In a way this Directive corresponded to the American Vietnamization policy. The North was itself trying to get the Vietcong back into the war. But the Vietcong in the populated areas were very much on the defensive and losing ground at an alarming rate — and, with it, their recruiting base. The North did its best to help. In addition to the fillers which had been coming into Vietcong guerrilla units, so that in most areas these now accounted for over 50 per cent of Vietcong unit strengths and in some areas as high as 80 per cent, political cadres were now introduced into the infrastructure. But, not being southerners, they were regarded as foreigners by the local population. To quote an extreme case of what was happening, I can remember asking in 1971 what had happened to a famous Vietcong company (316) in Long An province, twenty miles south of Saigon, which in the middle 1960s had been 200–300 strong and a very effective unit. I was told that it was now down to three men, all of whom were North Vietnamese.

By the end of 1970 therefore the Politburo was compelled to review its war strategy. There were really only two alternatives: 'more of the same' or a conventional invasion. Right up until

1972 several serious American commentators on the war were still forecasting the possibility of further Tet type offensives into the towns. These were out of the question and the Politburo knew it, even though the commentators did not. The Vietcong units to carry it out no longer existed, nor could the Vietcong infrastructure pre-position supplies and caches for the North Vietnamese Army to penetrate that distance and sustain such an offensive. It would have been suicidal, even more so than the later offensives in the summer of 1968 which had caused some of the highest ranking NVA and Vietcong defectors of the war (such as those mentioned in my abortive *New York Times* article). There was much to be said for 'more of the same' or, as it should be called in communist terminology, 'protracted war'. It was, after all, the orthodox doctrine. North Vietnam was not being bombed and the bombing of the Ho Chi Minh trail in the vast spaces of southern Laos could never decisively interdict the passage of reinforcements and supplies when time was no object. The 'rear bases' were, therefore, secure and the North Vietnamese Army could continue its harassing operations for five, ten or fifty years if necessary, thereby forcing the South Vietnamese to remain on a war footing and the Americans to maintain their aid and support. Meanwhile, the slow process of rebuilding the Vietcong, as expounded in COSVN Directive No. 9, could continue with every prospect that, at some point in the future, political or economic circumstances within the South might provide the opportunity for a more decisive blow.

But the arguments against this were stronger. This strategy would obviously take a very long time and even then its outcome was uncertain. The losses incurred over the previous three years, on General Giap's own admission, had been enormous. The NVA's morale, according to defectors, was low and to maintain the attrition strategy of 'more of the same' with an indefinite postponement of victory might have damaged it still further. The Politburo, therefore, was uncertain that the North could maintain protracted war effectively without serious risks of manpower shortages, economic stagnation and growing apathy to the war. There is enough evidence in their statements, decrees and broadcasts at this time to suggest that this was so. Instead of increasing over the years, therefore, the North's capability might have declined. This was equally true of the Vietcong in the South. The attrition rate was hitting them proportionately still harder and there was no evidence that a future resurgence, such as a repetition of their growth between 1959 and 1965, would be possible. All the evidence pointed in exactly the opposite direction.

In this respect the Politburo understood, even if critical opponents of the war did not, that Vietnamization and Pacification were working. The Russians also, in guarded comments in diplomatic circles, were admitting it too. It was clear that these two policies would continue to make progress through 1971 and that the withdrawal of American forces could be maintained safely at a rapid rate. About 200,000 had already left, most of the remainder were out of combat and there was no sign of South Vietnam falling apart. If this were to continue uninterrupted through 1972, Vietnam would almost cease to be a political issue within the United States and would have no influence at all on the American Presidential election. There was every prospect that the success of these policies would become apparent and give President Nixon a cosy re-election. The Politburo could foresee that in his second term he would be politically stronger and would have greater freedom of action, with the result that South Vietnam might achieve a situation in which the Vietcong were defeated in their revolutionary war beyond recovery, with no hope of the North Vietnamese Army preventing this or hampering further GVN progress in the populated areas through infiltration or raids. This prognosis was to be strongly reinforced later in 1971 by the improved economic situation within the South and the good harvest at the end of that year but, by that time, the decision had been taken.

There was another point which had to be taken into account —Cambodia and the loss of Sihanoukville. ARVN had taken part with recognized success in the Cambodian operation in the spring of 1970 and was continuing to operate within Cambodia, although with mixed results, both in support of the Cambodian Government and also against the lower end of the Ho Chi Minh trail between the South Vietnamese border in

Region III and the Mekong. With the loss of Sihanoukville, the North Vietnamese Army and the Vietcong in the whole of this eastern area of Cambodia, and in the southern part of South Vietnam, were logistically at their weakest, even though new trails were opened along tracks and rivers further to the west. The sheer distance over which supplies had to be moved and the high rate of sickness, mainly malaria, among the troops meant that only a very low level of operations could be maintained. Some of the more important traditional Vietcong base areas in the Camau, and in the coastal mangrove swamps of the Delta, were now several hundred miles from the original end of the trail in north-east Cambodia.[32] With American air and naval ('Market Time') operations being maintained, the chances of these forces being supplied by sea as before were negligible. For a period it even became local policy for units to revert to captured weaponry, for which they could obtain ammunition by attacks on outposts, because ammunition for AK 47s was in such short supply. Yet the whole of this southern area, because of its population density and production, was really the key target. The Politburo therefore found itself in a position where its main military strength could be applied more in the northern portion of South Vietnam nearer its own sources of supply, and much less against those areas which were the vital 'rear bases' of the GVN.

Into this argument between 'more of the same' or invasion there must be injected one further human factor. All the members of the Politburo were over 60. With Ho Chi Minh dead and his testament still not yet achieved, they felt that they could no longer rely on protracted war to achieve victory in their own lifetime. The unification of Vietnam (and it is interesting to note that in all their statements domestically they use the term unification not re-unification, which is only used for international consumption) had been their dedicated and determined goal for over twenty years and was the sole justification for the casualties and damage suffered and inflicted during the previous years of the war, for every act committed and indeed for their very retention of power. They were therefore old men in a hurry.

At the end of 1969, after seeing the initial success of Pacifica-

88

tion and Vietnamization, it had already occurred to me that, if the success of these programmes continued and if political stability and economic progress in the South improved, then by 1972 Hanoi would be left with the sole option of a conventional invasion. Requiring as it would the support of Russia and China, and inviting as it would a different response, such an invasion was not a course that they could lightly undertake. For that reason a future conventional invasion was not quite a forecastable certainty. There had to be still more compelling reasons than the arguments already set out. That President Nixon, with the full agreement of President Thieu, had adopted a winning strategy was not enough to compel such a drastic change of strategy on the part of Hanoi. If an invasion was to be carried out it had to have a good chance of success, either militarily on the ground or politically within the United States. Moreover, from the practical point of view, it would require exceptional logistic support from Russia and China.

At the end of 1970, looking back over the American scene of the previous twelve months, the Politburo had much to encourage it. After the moratoriums at the end of 1969 there had been the violent demonstrations over Cambodia in 1970. In subsequent statements and broadcasts the President had sounded apologetic and more defensive on the Vietnam issue. The failure of the Republicans to make any real gains in the mid-term elections suggested that, in view of his campaign effort, the President's popularity and standing were waning. The conclusion drawn by Hanoi was that he would be vulnerable in an election year. Just as they had succeeded in overthrowing the Laniel Cabinet in France in 1954, and President Johnson in 1968, so it appeared to the members of the Politburo that they could do the same again with President Nixon in 1972. In this respect it might be said that they were victims of their own history. They were further encouraged in this view by all the anti-war visitors to Hanoi at that time. If peace was the objective of these visitors they certainly went to the right capital; unfortunately they had exactly the opposite effect.

It may never be known on what precise date the decision to invade was taken. But it was probably at the end of 1970 or early in 1971. It was not of course an irrevocable decision

89

because it could have been cancelled at any time. In June or July, 1971, the actual orders were issued through the Lao Dong Party's Resolution No. 13. The Resolution reached COSVN in August, which then issued at least twelve implementing directives. The number of 13 for the Resolution is interesting because it was out of sequence but was probably chosen because the same number had been used for the Tet offensive in 1968. At least there can be no dispute as to where all the major decisions were taken throughout the war.

One further factor of military relevance had been provided early in 1971 by the South Vietnamese raid along Route 9, to Tchepone in Laos, under the code name 'Lam Son 719' and probably clinched the decision. In the first instance the very fact that the South Vietnamese were able to release such a force for an offensive operation into the North's secure 'rear bases' indicated that the balance of capability was changing. A country which has been under communist attack for twelve years is not supposed to be able to counter-attack. It is entirely contrary to doctrine that at such a point communist 'rear bases' should be attacked and does not accord with the communist view of its 'paper tiger' enemies.

The Lam Son 719 operation itself got off to a good start thanks to a spectacular engineering feat on the part of the remaining American forces in the area. The road west to Khe Sanh, except for the final bridge which took forty-eight hours, was repaired in twenty-four hours and the airstrip there was operating again. Bad weather then almost completely restricted air and helicopter operations for several days. Even so, the raiding forces made some headway. It was in my view a tactical error to have inserted the more lightly equipped forces, such as the Rangers and the Airborne, on the northern flank, on which the heaviest NVA response could be expected to fall, while inserting the renowned 1st Division on the southern flank where it was hoped to carry out the greatest destruction on supply dumps and the trail itself. Another error was to position the artillery fire-bases away from the road by which they could have been resupplied, so that all their supplies had to go in by helicopters which were vulnerable to weather and NVA fire. The raid certainly stirred up a hornet's nest and there were heavy casualties on both sides. On the way in, the South Vietnamese fought well. One Ranger battalion on the northern flank was practically decimated by repeated assaults. After receiving 200 casualties and inflicting three or four times that number on the enemy, it successfully withdrew in good order to a neighbouring position, with all its weapons and carrying all its wounded. There was no rout.

As with all raids, the objective was limited in both time and space. After causing as much damage as possible to supply dumps, the petrol pipeline and the trail, the time came to withdraw. A withdrawal in the face of the enemy is probably the most exacting operation of war, particularly after a raid. When a raid starts all the momentum is forward and units which get into trouble can be supported by those following. In a withdrawal, all the movement is in the opposite direction and any unit at the rear which gets into trouble is liable to be cut off with little chance of rescue. I have always thought it a good rule in conducting a raid to order the withdrawal at least three days before you think you should, otherwise there will be a scramble to get the rearguard units out. There was certainly a scramble in this case, the key consideration being to get the men out. The picture of a South Vietnamese soldier coming out on the skids of a helicopter was flashed around the television screens of the world for days on end. It gave an unfair and false picture of the fighting quality of the South Vietnamese troops. All I can say is that, when I took part in a similar raid during World War II into North Burma (the first Chindit operation in 1943) and we were ordered to withdraw with about 150 miles to go and the Irrawaddy and Chindwin rivers to cross, I would have given anything to come out on the skids of a helicopter. As it was we had to walk, and lost a lot of men on the way.

But the more significant point about the withdrawal, from the point of view of the invasion decision, was that in its closing stages the NVA was able to commit some of its Russian heavy artillery and tanks against the South Vietnamese rearguard with their lighter American tanks. Some heavy equipment of this nature had already been supplied over the previous few years by the Russians but this was the first time that it had really been in action. It was probably moving south down the

Ho Chi Minh trail as part of the contingency preparation for the later invasion. This action encouraged the North Vietnamese to believe that, given such weaponry on a much larger scale, they could defeat ARVN in battle and thereby win a military victory through a conventional invasion. It reinforced their conviction that an invasion was the right course to adopt.

On the South Vietnamese side, however, there were, as it turned out, a further twelve months for all the programmes connected with Vietnamization and Pacification to continue uninterrupted. Whether the Laos operation delayed the invasion cannot be readily assessed but, if it did so even by a matter of a few weeks (and it was certainly expected earlier than it came), Lam Son 719 paid off.

There were, therefore, strong arguments for discarding the doctrine of protracted revolutionary war and deciding to invade with every chance of success either military or political. There remained, however, one other factor—no invasion could be carried out without Russian and Chinese support. The majority of previous Russian aid had been defensive, particularly for air defence against the bombing of the North between 1965 and 1968. This equipment had ranged from MIGs and SAMs down to all forms of anti-aircraft weapon. Hanoi and Haiphong were at this time the most heavily defended cities in the world. Some heavy offensive weaponry had been provided for the NVA, including artillery and tanks, but most equipment for the army was of the type which could be carried by troops engaged in guerrilla type warfare from 122mm rockets down to AK 47 rifles. If an invasion was to be carried out, not only would more tanks and artillery be required but also more air defence equipment, both for the North's cities and communications against a possible renewal of American air attacks, and for the invading forces against American and South Vietnamese tactical aircraft and helicopters operating in support of ARVN. But more important still was transport, POL* and pipelines to keep supplies moving to the front. Gone would be the days when human porterage could meet the needs of the army. T54 tanks could not depend on gasoline carried to the front in water bottles. China could supply some of the

* Petrol, oil and lubricants.

needs, including food, but for the major weapons and the transport the agreement and assistance of Russia and other countries in the eastern bloc were essential. Accordingly, in the spring of 1971, Le Duan visited Moscow and stayed for several weeks.

Russia knew that by 1972 there would be serious problems to discuss and negotiate with the United States on Strategic Arms Limitation (SALT), Berlin, a European Security Conference, troop reductions in Europe, technical aid for Russian industrial development, as well as many other matters. It is probable that a poor harvest in 1971 had already been forecast, so that Russia would also be seeking large-scale cereal imports which could only come from the United States. Russia has at least always understood that, when it comes to tough negotiations, it pays to be bargaining from a position of strength. If President Nixon could be embarrassed by a flare-up of the Vietnam war or, even better, a defeat in Vietnam in a Presidential election year, he might be stretched over a barrel and therefore ready to make concessions on other issues in order to reach agreements which would look good in terms of American domestic politics. It therefore suited Russia very well to put Vietnam back into the headlines of the American press.

At the same time, with forty-four divisions deployed on the Chinese frontier as part of her containment of China policy, Russia could expect that her support for North Vietnam in its major requirements would give her the dominant influence in Hanoi, on China's southern flank, and subsequently in South East Asia if the invasion was successful. If, as a result of the invasion, a vastly expanded communist state was created in Indochina, it would need considerable Russian political and economic support in the initial stages for its survival (it had been the Russians who, by their trade agreement with Burma in 1955, had obtained the Burmese rice urgently needed to relieve starvation in the new communist state of North Vietnam). With the prospect of a complete collapse of American policy in South East Asia following a defeat in Vietnam, Russia could foresee a vacuum there which she could fill (the kite of a Russian-sponsored South East Asia security treaty had already been flown), thereby completing her encirclement and containment of China.

Throughout 1971 the stuff poured in. It included MIG 21s, SAM missiles, T54 tanks, the unrivalled 130mm guns, 130mm mortars, and, for the first time, SA7 heat-seeking missiles* together with spares, ammunition, trucks and POL in unprecedented quantities. Nothing occurred throughout 1971 to alter the decision. On the contrary, within South Vietnam Vietnamization and Pacification continued to progress, there was an excellent harvest, greater stability and prosperity than the South Vietnamese had known in the past. Within the United States the unopposed re-election of President Thieu in October, 1971, had further alienated the critics of American policy and the POW issue had given a fresh impetus to the end-the-war movement. All this confirmed the correctness of the decision. By the beginning of 1972 it was quite clear that the invasion was on.

* Missiles which are fired in the general direction of a helicopter or other low-flying aircraft, and which home on the heat from the exhaust.

CHAPTER VI

THE EASTER INVASION

The preparations for the invasion were quite apparent to the American and South Vietnamese commands. A warning shot was fired when President Nixon ordered a short period of bombing on military targets north of the DMZ and south of the 20th Parallel from 26 to 30 December, 1971, but went unheeded by the North. It was in these circumstances that General John D. Lavelle, commanding General of the US Seventh Air Force, subsequently exceeded his instructions and took the opportunity to use tactical aircraft, employed in a repressive role against NVA AA firing on American reconnaissance aircraft, to continue hitting supply dumps. It was an exceedingly frustrating situation for everyone concerned to be able to see the invasion coming without being able to take any pre-emptive action before it was launched. It was the oldest of dilemmas in this type of war. If you wait for the evidence, you then have a full-scale invasion (or other crisis) on your hands. If you act pre-emptively to prevent it and succeed, you then have no evidence. And if, which is more likely, you only partially succeed, the invasion is then blamed on the bombing.

Much time was spent by intelligence officers in trying to answer the questions, When? Where? and How Much? The initiative lay entirely with the North and only the Politburo knew the answers.

There were many commentators who speculated that the North Vietnamese might wait until 1973, by which time most, if not all, American forces would be out under the withdrawal programme. But in this respect, from Hanoi's point of view, 1972 was just as good because American forces by the end of January were down to 140,000 and were due to go down to under 70,000 by the end of April, with only three combat battalions left in the country and with greatly reduced tactical air force and helicopter support squadrons available. In one way this made 1972 even more attractive to the North because, if a military victory could be achieved, the Americans however

95

weak on the ground would be involved in the defeat. The possibility of a higher American casualty rate, and better still POWs on a large scale, was a juicy additional reward for victory which could not be ignored. For all other reasons also, as stated in the previous chapter, 1972 was the year.

The real dilemma for the North, as regards timing, was that the invasion must not be too early for the Presidential election in November, or too late for the weather. The monsoon rains at the end of May in the southern part of South Vietnam, while they would have little effect on the northern front, would hit the Ho Chi Minh trail and seriously hamper operations in southern Laos and Cambodia against South Vietnam's western flank. If the invasion was too early in the dry season, and failed to be decisive, it would be difficult to sustain the offensive through the monsoon in the summer and autumn as a means of influencing the election. On these grounds it could be predicted that the invasion would come some time between the middle of February and the end of March.

I was in South Vietnam during February and early March and all the indications were that the offensive would open on the tri-border front (where Laos, Cambodia and Vietnam meet) opposite Kontum in the last week of February. Probes were already being made and there were reports of considerable movement across the border including tanks. It is possible that the offensive on this front was delayed through logistic problems as a result of heavy bombing on the trail and some minor spoiling operations by ARVN's 22 Division. But by the time I left Vietnam in early March nothing had happened and the main concern was that Hanoi might delay the invasion until later in the summer which, while decreasing its prospects of military success in the South, would greatly increase its political prospects in the United States. I discounted this for two reasons: Hanoi wanted a decisive military victory and, secondly, it would have been difficult for them to keep their forces inactive so far forward for several months, both on logistic and morale grounds. The invasion would therefore come sooner rather than later. The end of March was really the deadline.

Where the invasion would fall was a much easier question to

answer because the position of the main NVA units could be calculated. There was clearly going to be a two-pronged attack in the north from Khe Sanh and across the DMZ (with 304th and 308th Divisions) and a right hook eastward from Laos border towards Hue (with 324B Division), with the objective of defeating ARVN forces in Region I, capturing Hue, the old imperial capital, and threatening the major supply port and air base of Danang sixty miles further south. A second thrust with 2 divisions (320th and 2nd) was also aimed at the Central Highlands, with Kontum as its first objective. Much further south in Region III the three NVA divisions (5th, 7th and 9th) could also be expected to make a thrust towards Saigon, either down Route 13 through An Loc or down the more densely populated route through Tay Ninh and along Route 1. Two other NVA divisions, the 3rd in the mountains in northern Binh Dinh province and the 1st on the Cambodian border south of the Mekong with elements in the U Minh forest, could also be expected to be active.

Once again it can be seen how difficult and inflexible is the problem of defending South Vietnam from attacks on all these fronts, when the choice of place and time rests entirely with the enemy. ARVN was stretched from the DMZ to the U Minh forest and it was essential not to commit any reserves until the weight of the thrusts could be assessed. While the main thrust obviously had to come in the north for reasons of closer re-supply and reinforcement, it could not immediately be judged whether the attacks in the Central Highlands or north of Saigon would be diversionary or major, nor was it certain which would come first or whether they would be simultaneous. As the weeks of March went by, clearly the time element was being telescoped and the likelihood of simultaneous attacks became greater.

But the real problem was the weight. It was easy to foresee that the invasion would result in battles greater than any seen in the world since Korea twenty years before, and bigger than those in the Six Day war. While a rough assessment could be made of the forces which would initially be committed by Hanoi (about 10 divisions with supporting arms totalling about 130,000 men) it could not be calculated how far these would be subsequently reinforced and therefore what the final commitment would be, or how long the offensive would be sustained. In a series of articles in *Nhan Dan* before the invasion General Giap, under the pseudonym of 'Victor', had called on the North Vietnamese for great sacrifices and a final effort for victory. I discussed this with General Creighton Abrams[33] and, in trying to assess the weight, we considered the number of casualties killed in action which Giap was prepared to take, i.e. 'the great sacrifices'. We reached the conclusion that it would be about 50–60,000 men. This again shows how the Western mind, even after being closely involved with this war for years, simply cannot fathom the ruthlessness of the communist mind when it comes to the expenditure of human lives. General Abrams and I were 100 per cent off. Hanoi was prepared to spend twice that number.

At 0200 hours on 30 March the invasion started across the DMZ and more or less simultaneously on the other two fronts: in the Central Highlands towards Kontum and in Binh Long province towards An Loc.

On the main northern front the first tactical error by ARVN was rapidly shown up; this was their reliance on static artillery 'fire bases', a concept which had been inherited from the American forces several years before. But at that time there had been four American divisions and one South Vietnamese division defending this front and there had been no major NVA invasion. Most NVA activity had been restricted to raids and incursions of varying strengths, but of seldom more than two to three regiments at a time. The same had applied in subsequent years up to the invasion. Even when the area was held in 1971 solely by the ARVN 3rd Division and a regiment of Marines, the infantry, supported by artillery fire from the fire bases, had always been able to deal effectively with any such incursion. Now, however, the invading forces had far greater weight with over two divisions (304th and 308th), supported by Russian T54 tanks and 130mm guns. This gun outranged the American 105mm and 155mm howitzers in the fire bases by more than six miles. It was also extremely accurate and, in the hilly open country south of the DMZ, forward observation of fire was excellent. The fire bases were literally blown to pieces, some of them like Camp Carroll, with a diameter of little more than three to four hundred yards across, taking over 2,000 rounds on the first morning. They were rapidly overrun by the following infantry and tanks. This soon pushed the ARVN front line back on to the Cua Viet river and the district capital of Dong Ha. The whole ten-mile strip between this river and the DMZ was lost within six days.

At the same time the NVA 324B Division operating from the Ah Shau valley on the Laos border began its attack eastward through the Annamite Chain towards Hue. This area was held by the ARVN 1st Division under Major-General Pham Van Phu, who first achieved fame as a fighting soldier when a captain in the French Union forces at Dien Bien Phu. The key defence position on this front was the old American fire base of Bastogne, which was to change hands frequently in the coming weeks. But as long as that area was held the 130mm guns could not reach Hue. Nor could the NVA, except in very small parties, threaten the communications leading to the main front further north. The fall back to Dong Ha coupled with the flood of civilian refugees from the border area, many of whom had originally come from the DMZ itself and had been living in new settlements along the border, gave the impression of a great NVA victory. But tragic columns of refugees shelled out of their homes do not represent the defeat of an army. They merely show the people's fear (remembering the massacres at Hue in 1968) of what might happen to them. Few of those reporting this flight at the time paused to reflect that an NVA gain of 10 miles in a week was, as I wrote in the London *Times*, 'not exactly an impressive initial thrust with 40,000 men and armour'. There had as yet been no rout. In fact there was something obviously wrong on the NVA side (there were frequent reports of tanks running out of gas) and a lull, if a continuing intense artillery bombardment can be called that, developed and lasted for three weeks.

The next front to become prominent was the southern front in Binh Long province, on the Cambodian border due north of Saigon, through which ran Route 13 to the capital. The district town of Loc Ninh on the border was lost early in April to the NVA 9th Division, which then pressed on towards An Loc, a small provincial town of about 20,000 people serving the large French rubber estates in that area. The town was cut off by 13 April and the heavy bombardment began. The first attack by the 9th Division and tanks was, however, beaten off. At this point the town, which was not strategically vital, might have been evacuated and there were good military reasons for withdrawing forces to better defensive positions further south. But President Thieu himself decided and announced that An Loc would be held at all costs. It was reinforced by elements of the 5th Division under General Hung and an airborne battalion which, when added to the Rangers and territorial forces under the province chief Colonel Tran Van Nhut,[34] increased the total forces in An Loc to between five and six thousand men. They were completely cut off and had to be supplied by high velocity parachute drops. Their wounded and a large number of civilians who had not been evacuated stayed with them. It was to become the symbolic battle of the invasion. On a smaller scale it was both a Guernica and a Stalingrad, and would have been hailed as such if the roles of the forces involved had been reversed.

Meanwhile, on the Central Highlands front, the battle had been slow in developing. This was a surprise. When I had visited the area on 20 February and saw General Dzu and the immortal John Paul Vann,[35] then senior American adviser in Region II, they had expected the initial attacks against Fire Bases 5 and 6 and other border outposts at any moment. As it was, not until 23 April did the main attack come on the 22nd Division with its forward headquarters at Tan Canh. This was overrun at night by NVA tanks[36] and the 22nd Division in full retreat fell back on Kontum. There was clearly no chance of their reforming to hold it in these circumstances, and the 23rd Division was rapidly brought up from Ban Me Thuot, 100 miles further south, and reached Kontum with only twenty-four hours to spare before the major battle for its possession began. The 22nd Division was pulled out altogether and reformed in Binh Dinh province on the coast, where it was given the task of recovering the three northern districts of Hoai Nhon (Bong Son), Hoai An and Tam Quan. When the invasion started the NVA 3rd Division, from its base areas in the Annamite Chain between Kontum and Binh Dinh, had sallied out into the coastal plain capturing these three districts thereby cutting Route 1 and severing all land communications to Region I and the northern front. Indeed, towards the end of April this, coupled with what was thought to be the imminent fall of Kontum and the consequential threat to Pleiku and Route 19 to the coast at Qui Nhon, appeared to be the critical front.

The widespread nature of these attacks was highly praised by many commentators as showing the brilliance of Giap's strategy and the flexibility of his forces.[37] The imminent collapse of South Vietnam was expected and the whole press was busy sharpening its knives-through-butter similes. But in fact the main battles had yet to be fought. It was my view at the time that the South Vietnamese would just make it but, as I told Dr. Kissinger, we would have to hold our breath. It was to be 'the nearest run thing'.

On an entirely different front the United States was recovering its nerve. It was a sign of the times that this Korean type communist invasion, which twenty years before would have prompted united Western action and ten years before a Kennedy crusade, immediately put in doubt American resolve and probably won the Wisconsin primary for Senator George McGovern. For a whole week retaliation was delayed before full-scale bombing of the North was resumed on 6th April. There was also fear of the political effect which increased American casualties might have. These had been running in single figures, or even zero, for every week over a long period as compared with the 500 or more in 1968; and even the possibility that they might reach double figures, if an American advisory team was overrun, caused the premature evacuation of such teams in somewhat shameful circumstances. This initially cautious response resulted in open friction with the South Vietnamese, and certainly did nothing for the latter's morale. Sensibly the issue was put on to a volunteer basis, as a result of which American advisers were able to stay with their South Vietnamese units. After all, good soldiers do not enjoy being ordered to desert their posts in the face of the enemy.

The second phase of the offensive opened at the end of April.

With the 325th committed the NVA now had four divisions operating on the northern front and its immediate western flank. Dong Ha was abandoned by ARVN on 29 April and this enabled the 130mm guns to open up on Quang Tri city. As thousands of shells poured into it the civilian population fled southwards along Route 1 to Hue. There then occurred a command snarl-up between Saigon, the Regional Commander (Lieut.-General Lam) and the Commander of the 3rd Division (Brigadier-General Giai), as a result of which the latter found his flank exposed and on 1 May ordered the 3rd Division to retire southwards. There has been much criticism of the 3rd Division, which was newly formed and had taken over from the 1st Division on the DMZ in the previous year. It had borne the full brunt of the initial thrusts and, before it broke, had held on at Dong Ha for a month against greatly superior NVA forces. By this time the full situation on all fronts was much clearer, and the higher command in Saigon was in a position to assess where and when to commit its reserves. Not many divisions would have stood up to the pounding which the 3rd had received, and it had already done its stuff and gained the necessary time. It was subsequently written off by most reporters as 'never to be heard of again', but in fact it was rapidly reformed and did sterling work in the Que Son area on the western approaches to Danang, against probes by NVA 711th Division in the later stages of the invasion.

Nevertheless, at this point panic set in. It was not just a case of the 3rd Division. There were all the territorial forces and the great majority of the civilian population of Quang Tri city and province, over 250,000 of them, all fleeing south into Hue, thereby triggering an exodus from that city also, so that refugees began pouring into Danang a further sixty miles south. There was looting and burning in Hue, but the press reports were much exaggerated and BBC radio (which is widely listened to in Vietnam) has been blamed for continuing to report a chaotic situation after order had been restored. There was one good cause for the panic, which was not reported, because at that time the press was not in a position to see it. On Route 1 south of Quang Tri there had occurred the 'act of calculated butchery',[38] when the NVA artillery blasted

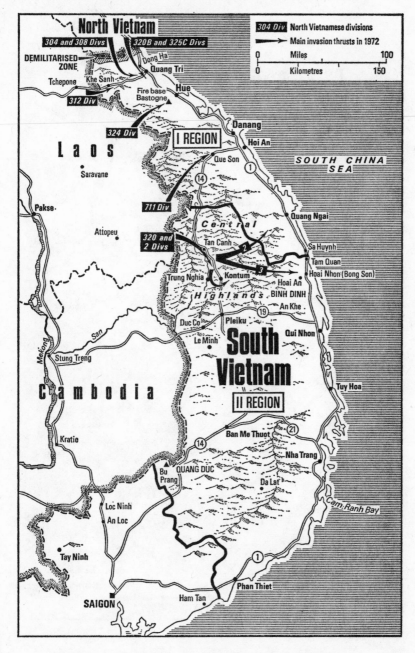

Map 2. South Vietnam—Military Regions I and II

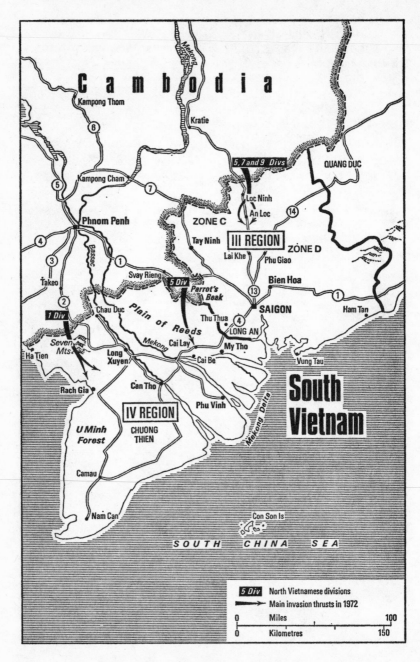

Map 3. South Vietnam—Military Regions III and IV

the columns of desperate refugees as they fled south. As already stated, it was estimated that over 20,000 were killed or wounded. The corpses were there for all to see when the area was later recaptured.

On May 2 President Thieu dismissed both Generals Lam and Giai and appointed Lieutenant-General Ngo Quang Truong to command all forces on the northern front. Previously he had been commanding the forces in Region IV (the Delta) and was regarded as South Vietnam's best General. Indeed, in my view, he is one of the finest Generals in the world today. He is in every sense a soldier's soldier, having risen from battalion and regimental command to command the 1st Division on the DMZ, where he gained a great reputation before being promoted to his Delta command. Within forty-eight hours of his arrival in the North, after having issued dramatic orders for the execution of deserters and looters, full control was restored, the forces were rallied, and new defensive lines were established on the My Chanh river 25 miles north of Hue. The Airborne and Marine Divisions from the national reserve were allocated to hold this front, while Major-General Phu with the 1st Division continued to hold the Bastogne area west of Hue. When I visited General Truong early in June the front was not only stabilized but he was preparing a counter-offensive to recapture Quang Tri, the second battle for which extended into July and August. By that time the NVA had six divisions on this front (304th, 308th, 324B, 325th, 320B and 312th). The 312th Division had been withdrawn from Laos and thrown into the battle with additional reinforcements of manpower for the remaining divisions. The three best ARVN divisions were more than a match for them.

Meanwhile, on the Central Highlands front everyone, including myself, had expected Kontum to fall. In the days of the Vietminh war the French had made no attempt to hold this provincial town sited in a river valley surrounded by hills with only one road, Route 14, running to the south, which of course could be easily cut. The town was now defended by the 23rd Division under Colonel Ba, and was soon surrounded and cut off by two NVA divisions (the 320th and 2nd) and other independent units with Russian tanks and 130mm guns. These began pounding the city, while sapper units about 1,000 strong penetrated the sprawling outskirts to occupy such vantage points as the Catholic Cathedral, the Bishop's residence, the hospital and an orphanage. On 25 May there was a two-pronged attack by the sappers inside the city and by the infantry and tanks advancing from outside. The battle lasted within the city confines for four days, but the 23rd Division held its ground and the attackers were forced to disengage, leaving their destroyed tanks behind almost buried in the rubble. The sappers were eliminated piecemeal in fierce house-to-house fighting. The NVA 320th Division retreated back to Tan Canh, which it continued to hold, while the 2nd Division moved back into the mountains north-east of Kontum to its old base area in Quang Ngai province, where it engaged the ARVN 2nd Division throughout the summer and autumn. On 30 May President Thieu flew in to Kontum to proclaim a major victory and to promote Colonel Ba to Brigadier-General.

There was an interesting sidelight on NVA tactics when they cut Route 14 in the Chu Pao pass, south of Kontum, before the battle. The NVA regiment, which had been given the task of harassing and blocking this road, used platoon-size groups to form continual temporary blocks. One section of a platoon armed with B40 rockets manned the roadside and was supported by a second section 100 yards in the rear to provide covering fire against ARVN infantry escorting the supply convoys. The third section with the platoon commander was placed a further 250 yards to the rear and was given the task of shooting the forward sections if they withdrew too soon. This emphasizes the difficulty which ARVN always had in clearing such forces from its lines of communication of which this, and Route 13 south of An Loc, were notable examples.

In this critical period at the beginning of May the battle of An Loc also reached its height. The NVA 9th Division having failed, the commander of the 5th Division proclaimed that, if he was given overall command of the 7th and 9th as well, he would take An Loc in two days. The city was finally pounded to rubble. Altogether over 70,000 rounds were poured in and, on each of the nights of the two main attacks on 11 and 15 May, over 7,000 rounds were fired. In a way this was a mistake, because rubble is comparatively easy for infantry to defend and is an obstruction to attacking forces, especially armour. The tanks were ordered in and rumbled into the heart of the town, often without supporting infantry. After the spectacular achievement of getting so many tanks so quickly so far south along the Ho Chi Minh trail, they were then squandered in An Loc. The first arrival of tanks, especially monsters like the T54 firing 100mm rounds, had been a shock to the ARVN infantry but, as soon as they found that their LAWs (light anti-tank weapon) worked, the men were queuing up to get them. In An Loc even the Police, having borrowed an LAW from the army, got one. On the final night the defenders of An Loc, now down to under 5,000, with their dead, dying and wounded round them, finally beat off the last attack by three NVA divisions. The symbolic battle had been won.

It was, however, still subject to sporadic artillery fire, and when I had the privilege of visiting the town in June a special helicopter operation had to be laid on by Major-General James F. Hollingsworth, the senior American adviser in Region III. With an escort of four gunships we travelled in at a height of 7,000 feet to reduce the risk of SA7 missiles and then spiralled rapidly down into the town. Because of the artillery fire, the chopper could only stay on the ground for fifteen seconds while we all leapt out and then drove round the town. There were practically no buildings left standing and certainly none undamaged. Wrecked tanks were scattered all over the place, thirty-nine of them within the town. When I described my visit on the following day to President Thieu he immediately asked for a similar flight to be laid on for him. The strictest security was observed and no announcement was made of his impending arrival. When he jumped first out of the helicopter the Province Chief, who was there to meet the party, broke down and wept. The troops in the surrounding bunkers, on seeing the President, rushed forward, lifted him up and carried him into the town. There were no press correspondents to see or report it.

While Quang Tri, Hue, Kontum and An Loc were the

major battles in the invasion and received the greater publicity, there were many other minor battles. In northern Binh Dinh the 22nd Division succeeded in recapturing the district towns of Tam Quan and Hoai Nhon and reopening Route 1, but failed to recapture the mountain district of Hoai An west of the highway held by the NVA 3rd Division. This limited success revealed the atrocities committed in that area while it had been under communist control. District and Village officials had been slung up by their feet and their throats cut and, as mentioned in my article for the *New York Times*, there was one case where forty-seven villagers were buried alive—and this in an area which was always reported by the press as being pro-VC. In the extreme south of the Delta the NVA 1st Division was exerting intense pressure in the province of Chuong Thien, particularly after the redeployment of ARVN 21st Division from that area to Route 13 south of An Loc. The battles were fought entirely by the local territorial forces and, although some populated areas were lost, no district town fell. This had long been a contested area, and in Vietminh days had been completely under communist control. Yet now it was holding out with its own local forces.

In support of their An Loc operation, the NVA carried out a number of regimental and battalion incursions round the Parrot's Beak into the border provinces of Hau Nghia and Long An. The normal feature of these operations was that the raiding force, say a battalion, would penetrate across the border and seize a government-held hamlet. In nearly every case the population fled to the nearest district town. Units of the local Regional and Popular Forces rapidly grouped for the purpose would then, with artillery and VNAF air support, drive the invaders out and back across the border. It was on one such occasion, when the population had fled from the hamlet, that the children were placed in a pagoda for safety, but several of them sneaked out to watch the battle. One girl was hit by napalm. It was a picture which shocked the world. But during all these battles in Hau Nghia province, out of 350,000 people only thirteen civilians were killed in the whole invasion period. The purpose of these subsidiary actions by the NVA was to draw off government regular troops, but in this the attackers failed and were themselves held or defeated by the Regional Forces.

In the Parrot's Beak area the raids were also intended to pose a threat to Saigon itself, and especially to Route 4 which was the rice and food supply lifeline to the Delta. But during the whole of 1972 traffic was never stopped for more than a few hours. As for Saigon, it was one of the incredible features of the whole invasion that no significant VC incident occurred in the city. In fact one point which came through very clearly from interrogations and captured documents was the Vietcong admission that they were incapable of assisting the invasion. In some areas they avoided action and even refused to supply guides to the invading forces. Partly because of this VC weakness the NVA, after their own failure at An Loc, withdrew the 5th Division for re-equipment and reinforcement in Cambodia and then despatched it to Kien Tuong province in the Delta, on the border between the Parrot's Beak and the Mekong. Here it was met and held by the ARVN 7th Division with the result that the heavily populated areas of the Delta were relatively unaffected by the invasion.

It will be noted that so far I have hardly mentioned American air support, because it is essential to emphasize first that air support would have been useless if ARVN had not held its ground and compelled the NVA to launch set piece attacks. In helping to break these up the tactical air support, and especially the B52 strikes, were quite devastating. The decision having been made on 6 April to commit the Navy and Air Force, there were no half measures. An enormous quantity of bombs was dropped in comparatively restricted areas round the points of attack. On all three main fronts the B52s played a decisive role. It must be recognized too, that both at Kontum and An Loc the defending infantry had no artillery support and were themselves being pounded by the NVA's guns. The air therefore was also being used in a counter-battery role. This was also necessary on the northern front, where only aircraft could get at the 130mm guns. Because in all the major battles ARVN was holding clear defence perimeters, it was possible for the professional soldiers arranging the air support to calculate the NVA's lines of attack and forming up areas. These could be accurately hit by the B52s from 30,000 feet, day and night, irrespective of the weather. On many occasions large bodies of enemy troops were caught before they had got into action; for example, at An Loc one column including fifteen tanks was engulfed in a B52 raid as it was moving in to attack the southern perimeter. The NVA constantly had to switch the position of its forces in an attempt to avoid being caught in such a raid. One obvious ploy was to move a unit into an area which had just been bombed, but since this could be deduced it was immediately bombed again. There was no respite. The NVA had foreseen the need to counter tactical air support and was heavily armed with all forms of AA weapons down to ·5 machine-guns. It also had the Strela SA7 missile, which could be carried and fired by one man, but these were only good against low-flying aircraft and helicopters. In all these battles the helicopter played a lesser role than in the past, partly because there were only about 1,000 available as compared with nearly 5,000 at the height of the American combat involvement. None of these anti-aircraft weapons were any use against F111s and B52s.

While, therefore, it is untrue to say that the battles were won solely by American air power, it would be true to say that they could not have been won without it. But even that needs to be put into perspective. As I wrote at the time: 'Excluding the United States, there is no single country in the Western world, given the shape and topography of South Vietnam, which could have withstood such an invasion without massive air support.'

The fighting quality of the ARVN soldier in defence, and the weight of American air power, were vital factors. So, too, were the mistakes made by North Vietnam. General Giap, having been brought up in the strategy of revolutionary war, made the fundamental strategic error of dispersing his forces in order to attack on three main fronts instead of adopting the conventional war strategy of concentrating his main forces to achieve a penetrating thrust at one point and to maintain momentum. The attacks on Kontum and An Loc, instead of being diversionary and previous, were in fact secondary simultaneous thrusts. It was exactly the same mistake as Hitler had made in his invasion of Russia. Both Giap and Hitler attempted to win on all three fronts at the same time, instead of selecting a priority front and ensuring victory at that point. If, for example, one or two of the divisions employed on the secondary fronts had been immediately available on the northern front, after the fall of Quang Tri on 1 May, the momentum might have been maintained there. Hue would have fallen and a total collapse might have followed. His dispersal of force resulted in momentum being lost on all three fronts. Of course, as with Hitler, one of the reasons for Giap's mistake was arrogance. He just did not believe that ARVN, faced with Blitzkrieg tactics and superior Russian weaponry, would stand up to the NVA.

Another effect of the dispersed attacks was to allow the South Vietnamese to commit more of their forces to the battle. The loss of momentum in the initial attacks gave the South Vietnamese time to move the Marines and Airborne to the north and to redeploy other divisions—the 23rd to Kontum and the 21st from the Delta to the An Loc area—in time for the decisive battles. Instead, therefore, of Giap's major thrust in the north falling with superior force on each South Vietnamese division like dominoes one after the other, the South Vietnamese were able to commit most of their regular divisions to all three battlefronts, thereby reversing the NVA's initial advantage and making fuller use of their overall superior manpower.

Giap's mistake was compounded by the tactics employed by his field commanders. Here there were two main errors: first, they all lacked the experience of co-ordinating attacks employing artillery, tanks and infantry. There was normally an intense artillery bombardment first which, while shaking the defenders, equally caused obstruction for the attackers. The tanks were then sent in unaccompanied by infantry, who were funnelled behind them and were therefore vulnerable to air attack. This misuse of tanks is interesting because over 3,000 North Vietnamese tank crews had had four to five months' training at the Russian armoured school in Odessa. They were evidently taught to drive and maintain, but were not taught the tactical use of tanks. For example, at An Loc if, after the spectacular achievement of getting so many down there, the tanks had by-passed the town with some supporting infantry, they would have been able to travel along a wide flat spur between the Song Be and Saigon rivers. This spur is mainly hard laterite and had plenty of rubber, scrub and other tree cover. It runs right down into the heavily populated area between Saigon and Bien Hoa. There they would have created complete panic and confusion. When General Abrams explained this to me, he said that any competent tank commander would have done it in forty-eight hours, to which I replied that Rommel would have done it in forty. It is the task of tanks to disrupt the opposing forces in depth, not to assault infantry dug into rubble with efficient anti-tank weapons in their hands. It is an interesting speculation that the invading forces might have been more successful if there had been no tanks at all.

The second error of the communist field commanders, having gained initial numerical superiority in the battle area, was to throw this advantage away in shock assaults in which the attrition rate was running at more than four or five to one against them. This led to a situation where the manpower balance shifted in favour of ARVN. This soon showed up on the battlefield after the NVA had taken horrendous casualties. Many of their battalions were down to under fifty men. There was evidence of desertions from units being sent to the front, and of hasty retreats from the battlefield leaving all their equipment behind—something quite unheard of in the past. One tank crew in Quang Tri actually bailed out and fled when they saw the Marines approaching, and the tank was captured intact with its engine running.

On the other hand, ARVN's numerical strength and fighting capability was increasing throughout the invasion. Over 84,000 recruits completed their full normal training through the months of May, June and July, which more than offset the casualties. Volunteers were so many for the élite divisions, such as the Airborne and Marines, that drafting was unnecessary for them. Meanwhile the United States were matching the Russian weaponry. M48 tanks, TOW anti-tank missiles and 175mm guns were pouring into Saigon together with large quantities of aircraft and other replacements.

Quite apart from these errors by the invaders there was also one serious miscalculation. From the preparations made for air defence, it can be safely assumed that the Politburo expected the bombing of North Vietnam to be resumed after the invasion started, but its members obviously hoped that, just as they had weathered the bombing attacks of 'Rolling Thunder' from 1965 to 1968, they would be able to do the same again. What they did not know about was the development of the new laser and television guided bombs with which the US Air Force was equipped. These 'smart bombs' were quite devastating in their accuracy. For example, during 'Rolling Thunder' between 800 and 1,000 sorties were flown against the Thanh Hoa bridge south of Hanoi and it was never hit. But now, in the first sortie of four Phantoms, it was hit at once by a 2,000 lbs smart bomb. Within a few weeks there was no bridge left intact. The road and rail communications from China, and between Hanoi and the northern front over nearly 400 miles, were particularly vulnerable. In addition warehouses, power stations, factories, repair facilities, radio stations and supply dumps were all hit. The accuracy of the new bomb allowed military targets to be destroyed which might never have been attacked by conventional bombs because of the risk of heavy civilian casualties. The most dramatic example of this was the attack on the Lang Chi hydro-electric power plant on 10 June. This is located about sixty-three miles north-west of Hanoi and was the largest power plant in North Vietnam, capable of providing 75 per cent of the country's electrical power. Five smart bombs were dropped clean through the concrete roof of the transformer house, destroying the turbines and generators without causing any material damage either to the dam or spillway ten yards away.

By drawing comparisons with the bombing campaign of 'Rolling Thunder' many people, in the United States particularly, were sceptical of the effectiveness of the new bombing campaign and failed to appreciate the very different circumstances which prevailed in the spring and summer of 1972. In October, 1972, the Senate Foreign Relations Committee actually issued a staff study based on the Pentagon Papers with regard to the effectiveness of bombing as a policy in Vietnam. As an opponent of the bombing policy in 1965 I had had to argue with some of its stronger supporters such as General Maxwell Taylor, Mr. Robert McNamara and, at a much lower level, Mr. Daniell Ellsberg. I do not question the conclusion reached by this staff study on the limited effectiveness of the bombing between 1965 and 1968 compared with its cost in all terms. To give it its due the study did make clear that it was based on the period 1965–68 and did not consider the current (1972) air war against North Vietnam. That, however, did not prevent individual Senators from drawing the same conclusions on the 1972 campaign in their public utterances.[39] They failed to appreciate that it was no longer a case of interdicting the intermittent and limited supplies required to maintain guerrilla-type warfare in the South, supported by NVA regiments and battalions infiltrating from secure sanctuaries in Cambodia; it was a full-scale invasion by fourteen divisions and 26 independent regiments (in its final stage)[40] with supporting armour and artillery, requiring vastly increased supplies and, what is more, requiring them on a day-to-day, not on an intermittent month-to-month basis. The consumption of POL and ammunition alone was running at several thousand tons a day. However well dispersed, such supplies always presented worthwhile targets along the whole communication network. Moreover, to keep them moving under intense and accurate bombing attacks stretched Hanoi's manpower to its limit. Also, in material costs in relation to results, the United States was paying far less than it did during the previous campaign. This also applied to costs in all terms, because the public at least understood what an invasion meant. The publicized effectiveness of the bombing certainly increased morale enormously in South Vietnam, which regarded the North as the enemy and saw no reason why the war should not be brought home to it. It was lowering morale in the North as prisoner reports testified. American determination and credibility were greatly enhanced, both because of their readiness to bomb and the technical efficiency of the bombing itself. This was particularly so in South East Asia, where at that time I visited most of the leading statesmen. One of them went so far as to say: 'I hope the Americans bomb that place until it can never make war on anyone again!'

American credibility was absolutely restored by the mining of Haiphong and other North Vietnamese ports on 8 May. It was quite clear that the mining would have no immediate effect on the battles which were then raging inside South Vietnam. There had after all been plenty of time over the previous year and even longer in which to build up stocks within the country to keep the war going for several months. The mining could only have a long-term effect, as opposed to the bombing which was more immediate. In this respect, therefore, it was complementary to the bombing and was aimed at reducing Hanoi's future capability to continue the war at the pace Hanoi itself had set. Moreover, the real threat was less to war supplies which could still be imported across the China border in limited, but still significant, quantities than to essential food supplies. Even in good harvest years North Vietnam has to import about 400,000 tons of cereals. That quantity can only be brought in by ships. The North had had fairly good harvests in 1971 and 1972 but shortage of food could be expected to have some effect early in 1973.

But that was only part of the purpose of the mining. A far more important purpose was the message which it conveyed to the Russians: 'If you arm your allies with superior offensive weapons to invade my allies, you must expect an appropriate American response which may involve you.' The Russians got the message at once. Communist ships in North Vietnam's ports made no attempt to sail and those en route to Haiphong were turned back. Russia was in no position in that area and at that range to make an effective reply. What is more, she well understood from the message that the American action was itself a response to what she had done and contained the added implication: 'If you escalate further, I will escalate further', which, after all, is the only way in which deterrence works.

Russia had never had any intention of allowing the Vietnam war to become a case for confrontation and certainly not at a time when there were vital matters to discuss with President Nixon at the Moscow summit within ten days. There was therefore no question whatever of the Moscow summit being postponed or cancelled as so many immediately predicted. On the contrary, it became even more imperative for Mr. Brezhnev to talk to President Nixon. It makes one despair of American politics that so few in the United States could see this. One Senator even went so far as to call the mining of Haiphong 'brinkmanship'. He was subsequently nominated for election to the Presidency.

Although the invasion was very costly no one can really call it a military blunder. It was certainly not a gamble, because there were moments when the North had been within an inch of total military victory. Nevertheless, not a single provincial capital, out of forty-four, had been captured and held (Quang Tri was the only one to be temporarily captured). Only half a dozen district capitals (out of over 260) in border or mountain areas were still held, which did give the NVA a more forward in-place position, with some control over territory if not of population. Because of the casualties suffered and the damage to communications in the North, there was, however, a risk developing that these gains might be lost, as Quang Tri had been, to South Vietnamese counter-offensives. There was no question of the North's offensive being renewed to gain political advantage just before the Presidential election. With Senator McGovern nominated as the Democratic candidate (perhaps for the North a somewhat perverse result of the invasion), President Nixon was clearly ahead in the polls and, on the Vietnam issue, by more than two to one. There was by September, therefore, nothing to be gained and much to be lost, both militarily and politically, by continuing the war at the current pace. Because of its own switch of strategy to conventional invasion, Hanoi was, for the first time, faced with a can-lose can't-win situation. There was, however, a good chance that by switching the war back to the negotiating table this might be reversed, the territorial gains held and some political gains made, provided that an enforceable peace could be avoided.

CHAPTER VII

NEGOTIATIONS

As I have written previously[41] there seem to be three circum-stances under which a communist revolutionary movement or government is prepared to negotiate: to secure international recognition of a victory; to prevent a complete defeat; and to open another front. The Indochina wars have provided examples of all three.

The negotiations leading to the Geneva Agreements of 1954 were primarily an example of securing international recognition of a victory, but there was also the secondary element of open-ing another front. The negotiations, which started while the battle of Dien Bien Phu was raging, opened another front be-cause the French will to continue fighting was already weaken-ing and the surrender at Dien Bien Phu, when coupled with the prospect of a settlement, completed this process. The French forces, if the will of the French government had not been broken, were by no means finally defeated and could have gone on fighting for several years. There was also the risk that the United States, which had been supporting the French with money and equipment, might directly intervene. The Vietminh (and their Russian and Chinese supporters) were therefore prepared to settle for what they could get from their gains on the battlefield, and so secured international recognition of their victory and the founding of North Vietnam as a new communist state without any reference to the ballot box.

In April, 1968, the talks about talks, or official discussions as they were formally called, were designed to implement the communist strategy of 'fighting while negotiating is aimed at opening another front'. These talks, leading to negotiations when the bombing was halted in November, 1968, were aimed directly at the erosion of American will to continue fighting, and indirectly, owing to anxiety and uncertainty as to American intentions, at the erosion of South Vietnamese will. There was no question of Hanoi making any concessions because, if it could be got across to the South Vietnamese people, whether true or not, that the United States were prepared at worst to scuttle or at best to accept a settlement which pre-determined a North Vietnamese takeover, the South Vietnamese will to continue fighting might crack. This in turn would have given Hanoi victory without the need for any concessions or further negotiations. This manœuvre very nearly succeeded in the last days of the Johnson Administration. It was stopped both by the election of President Nixon and by the staunch stand taken by President Thieu, who refused to act as an American puppet. Nevertheless, this 'another front' element in the negotiations, in which Hanoi's aim was the erosion of American will, continued for a further three years until after the invasion of 1972.

During this period of three years many peace plans, with a varying number of points, were tabled by all four parties and discussed. But as can be seen from the proposals both sides remained very far apart. The main points proposed by South Vietnam were that the North must give up its attempt to conquer South Vietnam by force and its forces must be completely withdrawn; the territories of Laos and Cambodia must not be violated; re-unification must be decided by the free choice of the entire population through the democratic process; and an effective system of international control and reliable guarantees must be established. The American proposals, while embracing these same points, offered also the withdrawal of all United States and other non-Vietnamese forces from South Vietnam over an agreed period, and the release of POWs by both sides. With reference to elections, President Nixon stated: 'We are prepared to accept any government in South Vietnam that results from the free choice of the South Vietnamese people themselves. We have no intention of imposing any form of government upon the people of South Vietnam nor will we be party to such a coercion. We have no objection to re-unification if that turns out to be what the people of South Vietnam and the people of North Vietnam want; we ask only that the decision reflects the free choice of the people concerned.'

In its counter-proposals the PRG, supported by Hanoi, insisted first on the withdrawal of all American forces by a certain date and, to make this more humiliating, offered to ensure their safety during the withdrawal. The question of Vietnamese armed forces in the South was then to be settled by the Vietnamese parties among themselves. The cessation of all American aid to the GVN was an additional part of the withdrawal requirement. The second main requirement was the establishment of a provisional coalition government. Originally this coalition was not to contain any members of the current GVN but was later modified to exclude specifically only President Thieu, Vice President Ky and Prime Minister Khiem. It would be this coalition government which would arrange and supervise subsequent elections in the South. Only after an agreement had been reached on these lines would a ceasefire be implemented. In other words, a political settlement in the North's favour had to come before a ceasefire.

Throughout the many sessions of the Paris talks two other persistent demands by the Hanoi and PRG delegations came through loud and clear. President Thieu must resign and the dual policies of Vietnamization and Pacification must be immediately halted. Why, if Thieu was such a catastrophe and these policies such dismal failures, as the critics of the war pretended, were the communist delegations so vigorously demanding their demise with almost every breath?

Of all the concessions made by the United States one in particular was a grievous error. This was the offer of a cease-fire-in-place with no time limit on it. The making of this offer was very strongly advocated by various members of the previous Johnson Administration, notably Mr. Cyrus Vance, who was a former Deputy Secretary of Defense and an earlier member of the American delegation at the Paris peace talks. All these advocates thought that it would bring an immediate acceptance from Hanoi instead of which, when President Nixon offered it in October, 1970, it was abusively rejected by Hanoi. (This was at the time of the mid-term elections and after the Cambodian operations, when President Nixon seemed to be on the defensive over his Vietnam policy.) The mistake lay in not putting a time limit on the offer, or in not withdrawing it after its rejection. One obvious reason for the rejection was that the North Vietnamese were not sufficiently 'in place' for the acceptance of the offer to be an attraction. As a result of the offer remaining open it was an encouragement, therefore, to get the NVA into place and, in that respect, was one of the contributory causes of the invasion in 1972. But, worse still, the continuation of the offer was the main reason why there could not be a successful ceasefire or an effective negotiated settlement in South Vietnam. Because the opposing forces would remain in place there could be no separation of forces, as after the Geneva Agreements of 1954, and therefore no chance of a real peace.

I was never against the offer of a ceasefire-in-place being made, if only to show that the North would reject it As a route to peace, however, I did consider that there were some obvious snags which few were ready to recognize: it could not be delineated; it could not be supervised; neither side would keep it; it would not end the war; and all the television cameras would be on the South Vietnamese side. These snags became all too clear in 1973.

When outlining his final eight-point peace plan in January, 1972, which still included the ceasefire-in-place (but throughout Indochina), the withdrawal of all American forces within six months, the exchange of POWs and a new Presidential election in South Vietnam, before which President Thieu would step down and resign, President Nixon also revealed that secret negotiations had been going on for the previous two and a half years between Dr. Kissinger and the North Vietnamese delegation, at twelve meetings, including seven with Le Duc Tho. These meetings continually foundered on the major point that the United States must first overthrow the government of South Vietnam. In the final stages of the secret negotiations towards the end of 1971 the North Vietnamese stalled, because by this time their plans for the invasion were well underway. When the eight-point plan was announced by the President in January it was flatly rejected by Hanoi for the same reason. While the secret negotiations went on, Hanoi had been able to exploit two issues to the full—the demand for a unilateral announcement of a deadline for the withdrawal of American forces and the offer, in return, to release American POWs. When Dr. Kissinger asked me why they had continued the secret negotiations for so long, I replied that the

North Vietnamese, with these two emotional pressure points at their disposal, were hoping that he would go just too far in his concessions and make one that would in effect cause the fall of the Saigon government and so hand South Vietnam to them on a plate.

Negotiations were suspended by the United States when the invasion started in 1972 but were resumed again in Paris on 27 April. The full American and South Vietnamese offers were again repeated (notably by President Nixon on 8 May at the time of the mining of Haiphong) only to be refused. When the Association of South East Asian Nations (ASEAN) — Thailand, Malaysia, Singapore, Indonesia and the Philippines — offered to mediate, their offer, forwarded by Hadji Adam Malik, the Foreign Minister of Indonesia, was rudely rejected by Hanoi and nothing appeared to have changed. However, by September, 1972, when the secret negotiations between Dr. Kissinger and Le Duc Tho were resumed, the whole situation had dramatically changed. The invasion had clearly failed in both its military and political aims, and there was no prospect of being able to renew the offensive in the immediate future. 'The great sacrifices' called for by General Giap had been paid to the extent of an estimated 130,000 men killed and disabled. All regular NVA divisions, except 316 Division in Laos, had been committed and the reinforcements being sent forward to the battalions in the South contained many teenagers with little more than a few weeks' training. Even with these, most units were well below half strength. Vast quantities of material, including at least half the 130mm guns and T 54 and other tanks, and possibly more, had been lost. There was considerable anxiety whether Russia and China (and particularly the former) would underwrite an invasion on this scale again or even make good the losses in view of President Nixon's successful summit meetings. The continued bombing of the North kept the damage, especially of communications, running at a higher rate than Hanoi's capacity to repair it. Further ahead, with the mining of the ports, was the problem of food imports in 1973. The spurious propaganda about the bombing of the dykes had rightly failed, since there was no flooding, to attract sympathy or to put pressure on the President, and

Hanoi could expect the accurate and relentless bombing campaign to continue.

For all this enormous expenditure and effort by the North the gains in the South were very minor. Not one single provincial town out of forty-four was in communist hands and only half a dozen district towns in remote border or mountain areas out of over 260 had been captured. Except in northern Quang Tri no real impact had been made on the populated areas, which remained firmly in Government hands. President Thieu's position and that of the whole government had been politically consolidated and the invasion had finally convinced the South Vietnamese that the North alone was the enemy. At no time had there been any sign of a mass uprising and no South Vietnamese units had defected. South Vietnam was in a much stronger political and military shape by September, 1972, than it had been before the invasion started six months earlier. There was the risk, therefore, that the gains made might now be lost and that a sustained counter-offensive by the South into the spring of 1973 might compel a limited NVA withdrawal to avoid piecemeal destruction of its units.

On top of all that, with Senator McGovern nominated as the Democratic candidate, it was certain that President Nixon was going to be re-elected in November. Moreover, while every American wanted an end to the war, President Nixon's policy of 'peace with honor' was finding far greater popular support than Senator McGovern's policy of abject surrender. If President Nixon could mine Haiphong on 8 May in an election year just before the Moscow Summit, there was no predicting what he might be able to do on 8 November after re-election. If, with both revolutionary war and a conventional invasion having failed, Hanoi remained completely intransigent at the conference table and continued to fight, not only were all its channels to victory, both military and political, blocked but there was the chance that further failures and the continued sacrifices would put the regime itself in jeopardy. For the first time in the Indochina wars the communist side was being compelled to negotiate in order to forestall the possibility of defeat.

While that had become the basic incentive to negotiate

seriously there was still the hope that, through fighting while negotiating as a means of eroding American will, the chance of future victory might be restored. In that respect Hanoi had reached three conclusions: that the war within the South could not be won politically through the collapse of the GVN but could in the long run only be won directly by military force or indirectly by military pressure; that it could not be won militarily while the United States, and particularly the United States Air Force and Navy, were still involved; and that, in the long term, the weakest link was the political will of the United States to go on supporting South Vietnam. In more practical terms at the negotiating table this meant that Hanoi had three main aims. Firstly, it was essential to get the American Air Force and Navy out of the war so that the damage in the North could be repaired and the ports re-opened. This would enable the North to repair its destroyed communications and the economy, and to build up again for later military activity. It would also relieve the manpower situation with fewer required to man air defences, repair damage and provide human porterage, thereby allowing the NVA to be brought up to full strength again. Secondly, it was necessary to safeguard the presence of the NVA 'in place' in the South, and the communications to the various fronts. This aim would of course be furthered by the removal of American tactical air support for the South Vietnamese. Thirdly, it would be highly desirable to impose as many restrictions as possible on any future South Vietnamese or American counter-action while leaving the North and the VC with few or no restraints on future activity. A perfect example of this was to be the restraining of the South Vietnamese from taking any action in Cambodia while the North still had a free hand there.

Looked at dispassionately these aims were in effect designed to achieve a fundamental principle of both insurgency and war in general — the securing of the safety of the North's 'rear bases', and its communications to the front, while maintaining the military threat to the South's 'rear bases' and its communications to the front. In other words, through the conference table, the North was aiming to reverse what it had lost on the battlefield and to restore a can't-lose can-win situation.

By July, 1972, it was not difficult to predict that Hanoi would make an offer and that the timing of it would be about the end of September. Partly as a result of the various summits and other high-level visits, there were already strong rumours that an arranged ceasefire was in the offing. There was, however, some divergence as between the two extremes of a limited ceasefire-in-place within South Vietnam only, and a supervised ceasefire on the recognized territorial boundaries throughout the whole of Indochina. I have already mentioned the weaknesses of the former and, with regard to the latter, there were as yet no absolutely compelling reasons why Hanoi had to accept such a drastic pull-back and thereby restrict her future options. The terms of a ceasefire seemed likely to be somewhere in between, but the key word in a ceasefire as part of any settlement was clearly going to be 'supervised'. With these considerations in mind, it was obvious that Hanoi's probable short-term intentions would be to continue the offensive, subject to the limitations of weather, manpower and supplies, as far into September as possible, hoping for some local success which, while militarily of little consequence, would at least hit the headlines and, at the same time, to infiltrate its residual manpower as replacements to traditional Vietcong base areas, especially those with access to the coast (because, after a ceasefire, they could be re-supplied by trawlers). It was my guess that Hanoi would then make a phony peace offer close enough to the Presidential election to keep Vietnam a burning issue but sufficiently in advance to make it difficult to stall, and that the offer might include a ceasefire-in-place and the release of American POWs, including possibly the actual release of about fifty to create the impression of good intentions. (In fact, Hanoi only released three.)[42] Although it would be a fundamental change in policy, Hanoi would probably drop its demands for the resignation of President Thieu and the cessation of all American aid, but would demand the withdrawal of the remaining American forces by about 1 January, 1973. There were, of course, possible variations of this scenario, but it seemed in July to be the likely manœuvre.

The breakthrough came on 8 October when Hanoi offered new and distinct proposals containing some substantive concessions. In order to get the maximum mileage out of these in the pre-election period in the United States, and to drive a wedge between the United States and South Vietnam, Hanoi prematurely, and contrary to an understanding, released on 26 October the general terms which had been substantially agreed in principle as if the text had been precisely determined and as if they had already been fully agreed in detail, which, of course, was not the case. At the same time Hanoi demanded the signing of the agreement within five days on 31 October.

From the end of October until the final signing of the agreement at the end of January, 1973, a lot of nonsense was written and spoken to the effect that the terms could have been achieved by the American Administration at any time during the previous four years. According to my calculation there were at least eight major concessions which had always been previously rejected. These were: Hanoi agreed to separate the ceasefire and the final political settlement whereas before it had always insisted on the ceasefire following after a pre-determined political settlement in its own favour. Hanoi agreed to a ceasefire-in-place in South Vietnam, which had previously been rejected ever since the offer was made in October, 1970. All four parties were to refrain from using the territories of Laos and Cambodia and to withdraw all foreign troops, which were mainly North Vietnamese, whereas in the past Hanoi had never even admitted the deployment of its troops outside North Vietnam. Hanoi agreed to the right of self-determination of the South Vietnamese people through elections under international supervision, whereas such an offer had always been abusively rejected in the past, even when it included the stepping down of President Thieu before such elections. Hanoi agreed to a National Council of Reconciliation to implement the agreement and to organize elections with participation by the present GVN, whereas previously Hanoi had always demanded a coalition government excluding the main personalities of the present GVN. The agreement allowed the GVN to continue receiving American economic and military aid, the latter on a replacement basis, whereas previously Hanoi had demanded that the withdrawal of United States forces should include the cessation of all American aid to

South Vietnam (while Senator McGovern had even offered to withdraw all major items of American equipment already given to South Vietnam). Hanoi agreed to the re-unification of Vietnam being achieved 'step by step through peaceful means' whereas re-unification by force had been the whole purpose of her war policy (and remains that even after the ceasefire). Hanoi agreed to an International Commission of Control and Supervision and to an International Conference on Vietnam, whereas the latter, or at least the reconvening of the Geneva Conference, had always been refused by North Vietnam, Russia and at times China.

As Solzhenitsyn pointed out in his *Open Letter to the Soviet Leaders*:[43] 'And as for wars being characteristic of capitalism alone and coming to an end when capitalism did—we have already witnessed the longest war of the twentieth century so far, and it was not capitalism that rejected negotiations and a truce for fifteen to twenty years . . .' A point that was widely missed by almost everyone was that Hanoi could have got these terms in 1970 except that at that time, as I have already mentioned, its forces were not sufficiently 'in-place' to make acceptance attractive. Hanoi might even have got similar terms as far back as 1966 when President Johnson first offered the withdrawal of American forces within six months. At that time the NVA was only partly in-place but the Vietcong decidedly were—they had not yet been decimated by the Tet offensive, and the subsequent Pacification programme. There was a deeper, but very simple, reason why Hanoi could not accept a settlement on these or similar terms much earlier. Hanoi had to continue fighting until American will had been so eroded that the terms of the settlement would not be enforced against the North, and continued American support for the South, after a settlement, would at least be doubtful. That condition was definitely not present in 1966 and was still uncertain in 1970. After all, just imagine the situation if the final terms had been fully enforced against the North, and the South was getting all the economic aid and replacement of military equipment it needed.

But, in the light of the North's seeming acceptance in October, 1972, of these previously rejected terms, it was not surprising when Dr. Kissinger stated at a press conference, after Hanoi's disclosure of the terms, that 'peace is at hand'. Containing as the terms did the offer to release all POWs, they naturally created a state of euphoric expectation within the United States in spite of Dr. Kissinger's warning that there were still a number of outstanding points as well as details to be worked out with regard to implementation, particularly with regard to the interpretation of certain provisions. The two main points at issue were the status and functioning of the National Council of Reconciliation, and the whole question of international supervision. The functioning of the National Council bristled with difficulties; it was to be composed of three equal segments — communist, neutralist and the GVN — in spite of the fact that the GVN was supported in its war aims by over 90 per cent of the population and the communists by less than 10 per cent and there was no definition of the neutralists or of whom they were supposed to represent. If they were the opposition in South Vietnam to President Thieu, that was now rallying behind him against the loose ends in the agreement. Each segment was to have a veto but there was no indication of what would happen if there was no unanimous decision. But, more important was the status. In the English language text it was referred to as an administrative structure whereas in the Vietnamese text it was called a government structure; and the Prime Minister of North Vietnam, Pham Van Dong, actually referred to it in a speech as 'a coalition government'. This was certainly not the intention of either the United States or South Vietnam. With regard to international supervision, the provisions were either vague or non-existent in relation to four vital issues: supervision of the ceasefire-in-place within South Vietnam; the withdrawal of foreign troops from Laos and Cambodia, where there was no coinciding ceasefire; one-for-one replacement of men and weapons within the South; and elections in South Vietnam. All these points were at the root of the trouble between Dr. Kissinger and President Thieu, particularly when the former was working from an English text which differed (as we shall see) from the Vietnamese text. It was President Thieu who had to explain the terms obtained to Dr. Kissinger, not the other way round, which did not make for an easy relationship.

Hanoi knew exactly what it was doing and, as always, the attacker held the initiative in proposing terms and fixing deadlines. The terms were intended to look attractive to public opinion in the United States, offering, as they appeared to do, an 'end to the war' and the return of prisoners. If Hanoi could not quite get South Vietnam on a plate, at least it could see that the plate was there and in place. That it was South Vietnam which would have to live or die as a result of breaches, abuses and misinterpretations of the agreement did not worry the appeasers and deserters who equated the withdrawal of the United States with peace, but it did concern the American Administration. The President, in spite of the imminence of the election, had no intention of throwing away in the last two weeks the points on which he had been standing for nearly four years.

Quite apart from domestic pressures, the President was also suffering from three basic errors in the American position. The first, which I have already discussed, was the outstanding offer of a ceasefire-in-place. This meant that the conflicting forces could not be separated on the ground and that a ceasefire would be impossible to supervise, even if the new ICCS had real teeth and was deprived of the supine chairmanship of the Indians. The ceasefire would at best be only temporary and full-scale war would break out again within months. Secondly, he had made the mistake of stopping the bombing north of the 20th Parallel as a gesture of good will. Such gestures gain no points in bargaining with communists. On the contrary, this gesture merely gave Hanoi a respite and took the pressure off. Thirdly, because of the breakthrough and the expectation of a successful conclusion to the negotiations, all forward counter-offensive planning came to a grinding halt. There was a general attitude of just maintaining the current military situation. In other words, on the American and South Vietnamese side the 'in-place' started in October, 1972. The lesson here is that, when negotiating with communists, all the operating pressures must be maintained at full force throughout the negotiations until a satisfactory agreement is reached and signed.

Hanoi made no such errors and in fact was going further. The major reason for the demand that the agreement should be signed on 31 October was that Hanoi was ready for it, whereas the South Vietnamese were not. All NVA and VC units had been issued with their instructions that, as soon as the ceasefire was signed, they were to launch a land-grabbing offensive. This intention was well known to the American Administration and was a major factor in its not being hustled into signing. The land-grabbing campaign went ahead regardless, for the simple reason that there was not time to stop it. It was a salutary lesson for the South Vietnamese in being prepared for a similar campaign when the ceasefire did finally come. In the event, the campaign proved very costly for the North Vietnamese and they made few gains from it but, coupled with the failure to maintain a counter-offensive strategy, it helped to keep the GVN militarily on the defensive when, for example, it should have retaken, as it could well have done, district towns like Loc Ninh, thereby helping to keep up the pressure on Hanoi to negotiate seriously.

The agreement was not signed on 31 October and the negotiations were resumed on 20 November. There were at least two good points: Hanoi could not now go back on the concessions which it had already made, and President Nixon's bargaining position was enormously improved by his landslide victory in the Presidential election. He could now force the pace but he first gave Hanoi every opportunity to reach this conclusion itself, instead of which it indulged in a 'charade' (or, as I had expected it to be, the offer was 'phony'). In a press conference on 16 December Dr. Kissinger explained what had happened in these subsequent negotiations. This is worth quoting at some length because it gives an idea of the problems of negotiating with a regime like that in Hanoi, and shows the difficulty of understanding whether Hanoi really wanted a negotiated settlement at all, or was just putting up phony proposals to achieve a political effect and to gain a respite:

'Now, let me say a word first about what were called "linguistic difficulties" which were called these in order not to inflame the situation. How did they arise? They arose because the North Vietnamese presented us a document in English which we then discussed with them. In many places throughout this document, the original wording was changed as the negotiations proceeded and the phrases were frequently weakened compared to the original formulation. It was not until we received the Vietnamese text, after those negotiations were concluded, that we found that while the English terms had been changed, the Vietnamese terms had been left unchanged.

So, we suddenly found ourselves engaged in two negotiations, one about the English text, the other about the Vietnamese text. Having conducted many negotiations, I must say this was a novel procedure. It led to the view that perhaps these were not simply linguistic difficulties, but substantive difficulties. Now, I must say all of these, except one, have now been eliminated. The second category of problems concerned bringing into being the international machinery so that it could operate simultaneously with the ceasefire and so as to avoid a situation where the ceasefire, rather than bring peace, would unleash another frenzy of warfare.

So to that end we submitted, on November 20th, the first day that the negotiations resumed, a list of what are called protocols, technical instruments to bring this machinery into being. These protocols—and I will not go into the details of these protocols—they are normally technical documents and ours were certainly intended to conform to normal practices. Despite the fact that this occurred four weeks after we had made clear that this was our intention and three weeks after Hanoi had pressed us to sign a ceasefire agreement, the North Vietnamese refused to discuss our protocols and refused to give us their protocols, so that the question of bringing the international machinery into being could not be addressed.

The first time we saw the North Vietnamese protocols was on the evening of December 12th, the night before I was supposed to leave Paris, six weeks after we had stated what our aim was, five weeks after the ceasefire was supposed to be signed, a ceasefire which called for that machinery to be set up immediately.

These protocols were not technical instruments, but reopened a whole list of issues that had been settled, or we thought had been settled, in the agreement. They contained provisions that were not in the original agreement, and they excluded provisions that were in the original agreement. They are now in the process of being discussed by the technical experts in Paris, but some effort will be needed to remove the political provisions from them and to return them to a technical status.

Secondly, I think it is safe to say that the North Vietnamese perception of international machinery and our perception of international machinery is at drastic variance, and that, ladies and gentlemen, is an understatement.

We had thought that an effective machinery required, in effect, some freedom of movement, and our estimate was that several thousand people were needed to monitor the many provisions of the agreement. The North Vietnamese perception is that the total force should be no more than 250, of which nearly half should be located at headquarters; that it would be dependent for its communication, logistics, and even physical necessities entirely on the party in whose area it was located.

So it would have no jeeps, no telephone, no radio of its own; that it could not move without being accompanied by liaison officers of the party that was to be investigated, if that party decided to give it the jeeps to get to where the violation was taking place and if that party would then let it communicate what it found.

It is our impression that the members of this commission will not exhaust themselves in frenzies of activity if this procedure were adopted.

Now, thirdly, the substance of the agreement. The negotiations since November 20th really have taken place in two phases. The first phase, which lasted for three days, continued the spirit and the attitude of the meetings in October. We presented our proposals. Some were accepted; others were rejected.

But by the end of the third day we had made very substantial progress, and all of us thought that we were within a day or two of completing the arrangements. We do not know what decisions were made in Hanoi at that point, but from that point on, the negotiations have had the character where a settlement was always just within our reach, and was always pulled just beyond our reach when we attempted to grasp it.

I do not think it is proper for me to go into the details of the specific issues, but I think I should give you a general atmosphere and a general sense of the procedures that were followed.

When we returned on December 4th, we of the American team, we thought that the meetings could not last more than two or three days because there were only two or three issues left to be resolved. You all know that the meetings lasted nine days. They began with Hanoi withdrawing every change that had been agreed to two weeks previously.

We then spent the rest of the week getting back to where we had already been two weeks before. By Saturday, we thought we had narrowed the issues sufficiently where, if the other side had accepted again one section they already had agreed to two weeks previously, the agreement could have been completed.

At that point, the President ordered General Haig to return to Washington so that he would be available for the mission, that would follow, of presenting the agreement to our allies. At that point, we thought we were sufficiently close so that experts could meet to conform the texts so that we would not again encounter the linguistic difficulties which we had experienced previously, and so that we could make sure that the changes that had been negotiated in English would also be reflected in Vietnamese.

When the experts met, they were presented with seventeen new changes in the guise of linguistic changes. When I met again with the special adviser (Le Duc Tho), the one problem which we thought remained on Saturday had grown to two, and a new demand was presented. When we accepted that, it was withdrawn the next day and sharpened up. So we spent our time going through the seventeen linguistic changes and reduced them again to two.

Then, on the last day of the meeting, we asked our experts to meet to compare whether the fifteen changes that had been settled, of the seventeen that had been proposed, now conformed in the two texts. At that point we were presented with sixteen new changes, including four substantive ones, some of which now still remain unsettled.

Now, I will not go into the details or into the merits of these changes. The major difficulty that we now face is that provisions that were settled in the agreement appear again in a different form in the protocols; that matters of technical implementation which were implicit in the agreement from the beginning have not been addressed and were not presented to us until the very last day of a series of sessions that had been specifically designed to discuss them; and that as soon as one issue was settled, a new issue was raised.

It was very tempting for us to continue the process which is so close to everybody's heart, implicit in the many meetings, of indicating great progress, but the President decided that we could not engage in a charade with the American people.

We are now in this curious position: great progress has been made, even in the talks. The only thing that is lacking is one decision in Hanoi, to settle the remaining issues in terms that two weeks previously they had already agreed to.

So, we are not talking of an issue of principle that is totally unacceptable.

Secondly, to complete the work that is required to bring the international machinery into being in the spirit that both sides have an interest of not ending the war in such a way that it is just the beginning of another round of conflict. So, we are in a position where peace can be near, but peace requires a decision. This is why we wanted to restate once more what our basic attitude is.

With respect to Saigon, we have sympathy and compassion for the anguish of their people and for the concerns of their government. But if we can get an agreement that the President considers just, we will proceed with it.

With respect to Hanoi, our basic objective was stated in the Press conference of October 26th. We want an end to the war that is something more than an armistice. We want to move from hostility to normalization and from normalization to co-operation. But we will not make a settlement which is a disguised form of continued warfare and which brings about, by indirection, what we have always said we would not tolerate.

We have always stated that a fair solution cannot possibly give either side everything that it wants. We are not continuing a war in order to give total victory to our allies. We want to give them a reasonable opportunity to participate in a political structure, but we also will not make a settlement which is a disguised form of victory for the other side.

Therefore, we are at a point where we are again perhaps closer to an agreement than we were at the end of October, if the other side is willing to deal with us in good faith and with good will. But it cannot do that if every day an issue is settled a new one is raised, that when an issue is settled in an agreement, it is raised again as an understanding and if it is settled in an understanding, it is raised again as a protocol. We will not be blackmailed into an agreement. We will not be stampeded into an agreement, and, if I may say so, we will not be charmed into an agreement, until its conditions are right.'[44]

The 'charade' was ended on the night of 18 December when bombing raids north of the 20th Parallel were resumed and, for the first time in that area, B52s were used. Although the ports were still closed by the mining, Hanoi had fully exploited the respite, as it was fully entitled to do if it wished to continue the war, by bringing in increased supplies through China and trucking them south to the front. The primary intention of the raids was to restore the situation to what it had been before the gesture of good will was made in October. After twelve days of intensive strikes by B52s, F111s and Phantoms which ended on the night of 29 December, it was reported[45] that:

'Virtually all industrial capacity was gone. Power generating plants and their transmitting grids were smashed. Gas and oil storage dumps were burned-out shells. Railroad marshalling yards looked like lunar landscapes. Roads and canals were clogged with shattered transport. SAM (surface-to-air missile) storage areas, tank, artillery and truck parks were pulverized. Military traffic dwindled to a trickle.'

Intensive and devastating though the raids were, they were also carried out against the most intensive air defences until then seen in war. B52 losses reached their peak on the third and fourth days when six were lost. But the defences then began to sag and for two days there were no losses. By 28 December the North's defences were shattered and the B52s, if the bombing had not stopped on the following day, would have been able to roam over the North with impunity. Hanoi was no longer able to track them with radar, its MIG21s could no longer get off to intercept them, and the re-supply of SAMs was only a fraction of their expenditure in the first few days of the raids (1,242 SAMs were fired in eleven days). The whole system was breaking down, including radio communications on which a communist regime is particularly dependent for control. At this point the war could have been won, in that a real and enforceable peace could have been obtained.

These raids gave rise to the wildest allegations of terror and carpet bombing of civilian targets, which were quite unjustified except for those who make a habit of employing double standards. I was given a full briefing on the raids when I visited Saigon in January, 1973. I was surprised at the lengths to which the United States Air Force had gone to ensure hitting military targets and avoiding civilian areas, at greatly increased risks to both aircraft and crews. Admittedly, there were three bad accidents, including the hitting of Bach Mai hospital adjacent to and just north of Bach Mai airfield. In the prevailing conditions of the air war it is surprising that there were not more. In fact, the greatest civilian damage was done by one B52 which crashed down a street in the centre of the city but not even Hanoi claimed that this was intentional. According to Hanoi's own estimates the number of civilians killed was between 1,300 and 1,600 over eleven days. While everyone should regret even a fraction of that figure, the credit for such a low figure goes entirely to the United States. The Luftwaffe killed that number in a single night (Coventry) in what must now be regarded as the comparatively mild bombing of British cities in the early years of the war. The RAF killed twenty to forty times that number in a single night in the fire-storm bombing of German cities. But the better comparison is with the North Vietnamese themselves. The toll was about the same as the number of civilians killed by the indiscriminate NVA artillery bombardment of An Loc in April and May, and one-fifth the number of refugees intentionally killed when fleeing from Quang Tri. Not one critic mentioned these, or Hue. They had all retreated into what George Orwell called 'the mental slum' of atrocity storymongering.

There were still some who questioned whether the bombing did break the deadlock in the ceasefire talks, but the POWs in Hanoi had no doubts on this score at all.[46] They knew instinctively that their release was imminent. Suffice it to say that agreement was quickly reached in Paris on both the text and outstanding points of the agreement and its implementing protocols, and the first ceasefire came into effect with a bang in South Vietnam at 8 a.m. on Sunday, 28 January, 1973.

CHAPTER VIII

THE CEASEFIRE

The signing of the agreement created the false impression that the ceasefire had ended the war. This fallacy had, in turn, been created over the years by those who, again falsely, blamed the war and its continuation on the presence of American forces in Vietnam. From Hanoi's point of view the agreement did not, nor was it intended to, end the war. Instead it gained for Hanoi an immediate respite which would enable the damage to the North, especially its communications and distribution system, to be repaired, its ports to be re-opened and all its depleted regular forces outside North Vietnam to be reinforced, re-supplied and re-equipped. In the longer term it had got the United States out of the day-to-day war, at least to the extent that their direct involvement could influence the military activity which would continue. More important, the agreement contained certain built-in advantages for the North Vietnamese with corresponding restraints on the South Vietnamese which would favour Hanoi in the 'difficult, complex and violent struggle ahead', as it was called in an NVA Order of the Day immediately after the ceasefire.

The point was that President Nixon, having gained a dominant bargaining position when the bombing halted on 29 December, 1972, could not press his advantage because antagonism to the bombing itself, and the very fact of his strong bargaining position, brought him under increased pressure in Congress and in the United States to accept a ceasefire on any superficially acceptable terms which would immediately end direct American involvement. As a result he could not press demands for concessions that really would have ended the war, such as the withdrawal of the NVA back into North Vietnam. Nor could he obtain, except on a piece of paper, the supervisory machinery to enforce an agreement. A real and lasting peace could only have been achieved at this point if he had been in a sufficiently strong position, in terms of American will, to threaten the continuation of the war and of the bombing and

137

mining for as long as necessary through 1973. Hanoi simply could not have faced this prospect. The North's whole war logistic and internal distribution system, and with it possibly administrative control, would have broken down. Moreover, as revealed at the beginning of 1974, the North had to import one million tons of cereals through 1973 (over three months' supply on the current ration) and therefore, to avoid the threat of starvation, itself needed a ceasefire on almost any terms which would allow its ports to be re-opened. But to continue the war was out of the question and the President could not even promote a mood of determination within the States to see that the terms of the ceasefire agreement were enforced. As a result the war in Indochina was to continue, though initially at a lower level, and thousands more lives were to be lost, all because a vocal short-sighted element in the United States did not want peace. They wanted OUT. Hanoi knew this and the United States and the West, not to mention the people of South Vietnam and Cambodia, are now paying for it. The eventual price may be higher still.

President Nixon was therefore compelled to accept terms because they coincided, at least on paper, with the terms previously laid down as representing 'peace with honor'. Even so, if these terms had been meticulously kept or had been enforceable, there would have been an end to the war and 'peace with honor'. South Vietnam's independence would have been invulnerable after elections under the agreement if these could have been held within the first year or two to determine the will of the South Vietnamese people. There would have been no need for simultaneous ceasefires in Cambodia or Laos, because these would have followed automatically if the terms of the agreement had been kept by the North with regard to the vital provision of Article 20, that there should be no foreign troops in either of these territories. South Vietnamese independence would have been doubly insured if the other vital provision of the agreement could have been enforced. This provided that, with regard to troops and equipment within the South, the NVA could only introduce a one-for-one replacement, i.e. that the total number of effective troops or weapons could not be increased after the ceasefire. But neither of these two vital provisions were enforceable against Hanoi without the machinery and, above all, without the will to enforce them.

Although Hanoi appeared to agree in principle to international supervision, it was only agreeing provided that the supervision did not work. In fact, in the original terms published by Hanoi in October, 1972, there was no provision at all for the international supervision mentioned in the terms and, in the final agreement and its related protocols, the supervision which was established operated solely against South Vietnam and the United States. As could be seen at once from the provisions relating to the International Commission of Control and Supervision (ICCS) the unanimity rule, with regard to reporting on and investigating violations of the ceasefire, would render the Commission futile and so it proved to be in practice. The Canadian and Indonesian delegations could be blocked on every occasion by the Poles and Hungarians. No investigations by individual members could be carried out and, when some Canadian officers tried, they were captured and treated as prisoners for several days. Even investigations by the Commission as a whole were easily discouraged if only by the shooting down of its helicopters. When shots or mortars were fired in the proximity of an ICCS team site, the Poles and Hungarians immediately deserted their post. By early 1974, in some of the more sensitive areas, only the Indonesian representatives remained. On one occasion, after a mortar bomb was fired into a school on 9 March, 1974, killing at least twenty-three South Vietnamese children, the PRG accused the Indonesian delegation of violating the Ceasefire Agreement because it carried out unilateral investigations at the request of the GVN. The Indonesian delegation rejected the allegation and blamed the Polish and Hungarian delegations for their negative attitude and for refusing to discharge the duties of the ICCS.

When the Commission failed to operate, it was not surprising that the Canadians pulled out, after their experience of the futility of the previous ICC (established by the Geneva Agreements of 1954). When Ambassador Michel Gauvin, the head of the Canadian delegation, departed, he said that the most serious violation of the ceasefire agreement had been North

Vietnam's disrespect for the neutrality of Laos and Cambodia and that allegations of North Vietnamese infiltration into South Vietnam since the ceasefire had been 'pretty substantially supported'. Commenting on his country's decision to pull out, he added that the ICCS had failed to function effectively and blamed this on the failure of 'some parties to the ceasefire agreement to live up to their commitment'. He made it very clear that he was referring to North Vietnam and the Vietcong.

The restrictions on South Vietnam were, however, as near absolute as they could be made. The South was fully open to public scrutiny of its every action through television cameras and, just after the ceasefire, one of the largest posses of reporters ever seen, many of them hostile and ready to report any misdemeanour. In spite of this the GVN welcomed visitors including politicians, even though they might be unsympathetic (for example, a British Labour Party delegation). The restraints on South Vietnam were imposed not by Poles and Hungarians but by South Vietnam's need for continued United States economic aid and military assistance (on a one-for-one basis as allowed by the agreement). For the purpose of enforcing the agreement against Saigon, Hanoi did not need Poles and Hungarians when it had Senator Fulbright and the Foreign Relations Committee of the United States' Senate.

The aftermath of the ceasefire was therefore quite predictable. On the morning that it took effect I was in Saigon and had arranged to visit Pleiku in the Central Highlands. Departure from Tan Son Nhut airport in Saigon was delayed for an hour or two owing to in-coming rockets and we eventually arrived at Pleiku to find that the same was occurring there. After all, if Russian 122mm rockets have been transported all that way to within reach of their target, it would have been a pity not to fire them. But the more interesting violations were the land grabbing and road blocking. The land grabbing had been fully expected and the South Vietnamese on this occasion were well prepared. South Vietnamese flags were much in evidence not only over every village house but even on the tops of palm trees round the rice fields. This was not designed to delineate territory but was more a psychological move to indicate solidarity. The most significant point was, however, that the land grabbing did not start, as might have been expected, several days before the ceasefire but during the night of the ceasefire and on the following days. The reason for this was that the NVA and VC units in the proximity of South Vietnamese controlled populated areas were too weak to mount a more sustained campaign as had occurred in October. Another significant point was that much of the land grabbing was no more than the establishment of road blocks in unpopulated areas, because many communist units lacked the strength to take on the Regional and Popular Forces defending the hamlets. By establishing a road block they hoped to be able to claim a right to their permanent presence at that point and thereby to cut off government controlled populated areas further along the road.

There were only a few major actions. Just before the ceasefire the South Vietnamese Marines attempted to gain a post at the mouth of the Cua Viet river in Quang Tri province. This would have been useful as a means of blocking the NVA's resupply by sea on the right flank of the northern front. But the Marines were driven out by the NVA on the days following the ceasefire. The NVA on the other hand was more concerned that it could not provide for the Provisional Revolutionary Government (PRG) either a capital or a port within South Vietnam. An attempt was made to capture the province capital of Phan Thiet on the coast about 100 miles north-east of Saigon, but this was comparatively easily beaten off. The two more serious attacks were on Tay Ninh, the sprawling provincial capital north-west of Saigon close to the Cambodian border, and on the fishing village of Sa Huynh in southern Quang Ngai province on the boundary between Military Regions I and II.

At Tay Ninh about 1,000 men from local Vietcong units, composed almost entirely of NVA fillers, attacked the eastern and southern outskirts of the town and cut Route 1 to Saigon. A confused battle in the suburbs lasted for two or three days until the attackers were thrown out with the loss of over 300 killed. Regular forces of both the NVA and ARVN were hardly engaged. The town was defended by the Regional

Forces (RF), Popular Forces (PF) and the local Peoples Self-Defence Forces (PSDF) under the province chief. The population itself turned out to support its own men by evacuating wounded, providing tea and food and directing the fire, even if it was at their own houses which had been occupied by the enemy. Of more importance was the carrying of the battle into the grounds of the famous Cao Dai temple, which brought the wrath of the whole Cao Dai sect down on the NVA and the VC, with the Cao Dai Pope himself condemning their action and pledging support to President Thieu. The PRG delegation to the Four Party Joint Military Commission[47] flying by Air France from Paris asked to be diverted over Tay Ninh on their way to Saigon so that they could admire the PRG flag flying over their new capital. But they were disappointed to find the town firmly in Government hands and South Vietnamese flags waving strongly in the wind.

At Sa Huynh the South Vietnamese were definitely caught napping. The fishing village itself is of little account but it did command a cove which could have been used by small seagoing trawlers of a few hundred tons. More important, a spur of the Annamite Chain runs right down to the sea at this point so that there is no coastal plain. The main north–south road (Route 1) and the railway line have been carved out of the cliff-side and go through a number of small passes. The NVA 2 Division threw in four battalions with instructions to take the village and hold it at all costs. The village was quickly overrun, though the Popular Force platoon defending it managed to hold out on a neighbouring hill for some time. The road north and south of the village over several miles was cut and held, thereby physically cutting off Military Region I in the north from all land communication with the rest of South Vietnam. The battle raged for several weeks until ARVN 2 Division under Brigadier General Nhut, the former province chief at An Loc, recaptured the area and cleared the road.

Although regular forces had to be used to clear some of the road blocks, the 319 hamlet-grabbing attempts, except in about half a dozen cases, were all repulsed by local forces. In one such Catholic hamlet, in a newly developed area on Route 1 about fifty miles north of Saigon, a Vietcong unit attempted to enter, after the ceasefire, only to be met by the village priest pointing at his watch and demanding their withdrawal. When they refused he called up all the villagers and asked them to vote by a show of hands as to whether they wished to be Government controlled or Vietcong controlled. The vote for the Government was unanimous and the Vietcong withdrew. In all other cases they fought to get in and were thrown forcefully out. Few of the attacks were pressed with the usual NVA and VC determination and, in the example quoted in Chapter I,* many of the attackers were convalescents hauled out of hospitals in Cambodia for the occasion.

The main GVN violations of the agreement, while these attacks were going on, were the shelling and continued bombing of NVA-held areas in the rear of the NVA attacking forces. Because this was their only response and not ground counteroffensives the expenditure of ammunition was phenomenal. Under Article 7 of the agreement it was of course all replaceable. In the final analysis, the position prevailing in the week before the ceasefire was largely restored and, if the ceasefire was to have any chance at all, it was that position which had to be recognized by all parties as 'in place'.

For the future, however, there was a much more serious violation than the post ceasefire land-grabbing attempts; this was the breach of Article 7 by the NVA. Aerial photography revealed that the North quite openly began to pour in additional troops and equipment well beyond a one-for-one replacement. There was a very good reason for this. With no hope of the PRG being able to gain any sort of political or election victory (this was even clearer at the beginning of 1974, by which time, inside South Vietnam, the PRG and VC were of no account at all) any future decision in Hanoi's favour could only be gained by direct military action or through military pressure. But, at the time of the ceasefire, the NVA in the South was so weakened by losses from the 1972 invasion and the subsequent land-grabbing operations that it needed a complete build-up just to restore a military threat to South Vietnam. No time was wasted and, as soon as communications were repaired, men and supplies poured in. Even SAMs were introduced at Khe

* See page 16.

Sanh and a new airstrip capable of taking MIG 21s was built, all of which was contrary to the agreement. Other airfields in occupied territory down the Laos border were also repaired, mainly for air supply outside any possible control by the ICCS and in flagrant violation of Article 7. There were only five nominated control points down the whole of the border for NVA one-for-one replacement of troops and equipment, all of which could be circumvented. Only one, Duc Co on the old Route 19 running from Pleiku to the Cambodian border, was in NVA hands and therefore an embarrassment. But, by failing to provide suitable accommodation and facilities, the ICCS team there was soon persuaded to leave. Life in a South Vietnamese city was more comfortable. The border was wide open with no supervision or control. It was also quite inaccessible to a keen reporter even if there was one.

There were three key areas. Hanoi had to rebuild its threat on the northern front, particularly from the Laos flank towards Hue, which was less overt and less easily supervised, in order to compel the GVN to keep its reserve Marine and Airborne divisions committed to Region I. In the Central Highlands (Region II) there was a steady build-up opposite Pleiku and Kontum, especially at first against the latter. This culminated six months after the ceasefire in the capture of the village of Trung Nghia across the Poko river, west of Kontum which had been the ceasefire line. This blatant breach of the agreement gave the NVA a bridgehead with an unobstructed run of only five miles to Kontum, thereby compelling ARVN 23 Division to adopt fixed and inflexible defence positions round the city. Similarly, in September, the Ranger post of Le Minh covering the western approaches to Pleiku was overrun by a major conventional assault, again causing ARVN to adopt a more defensive posture to protect populated areas and road communications. All this was intended to give the NVA a clear run through the vast unpopulated areas of the Annamite Chain for the infiltration of reinforcements and supplies to its two divisions (2 and 3) on the boundary between Military Regions I and II in southern Quang Ngai and northern Binh Dinh. By July, when I had again visited Vietnam, the NVA road building through the mountains for this purpose was very apparent from the air. This was part of the 'cut South Vietnam in half' strategy which was always one of the major threats throughout the war.

However, by early 1974 the position in Military Region II had been restored to the ceasefire situation. In Binh Dinh province the NVA 3 Division remained so weak that the security of the province could be left entirely to provincial forces supported by two Ranger groups. The whole of ARVN 22 Division was redeployed to Pleiku and Kontum and immediately relieved NVA pressure on both these towns. When I visited Kontum in February, 1974, only one regiment (instead of the whole 23 Division) plus local forces was needed to defend the area. 80,000 refugees had returned, houses were being rebuilt and the vegetable gardens on the former battlefield within the city were some of the best cultivation I have ever seen (a cabbage I bought weighed nearly 5 lbs). The situation west of Pleiku had also been stabilized in spite of the introduction of Russian 152mm guns. Le Minh had been re-entered but was in fact occupied by neither side. ARVN was learning to adopt a mobile role on its feet more suited to the vast jungle expanses on this front—a role which the US Army itself had never learnt.

But, if any real political pressure was to be worked up, the NVA's military threat to Saigon itself had to be restored. The sanctuaries along the Cambodian border and in Zone C north of Tay Ninh were therefore reactivated. 5 Division was brought back from the northern Mekong Delta to rejoin 7 and 9 Divisions and all three were reinforced. Stuff poured into this area during the remainder of the 1973 dry season, including tanks and, for the first time so far south, 130mm guns. Convoys of trucks were happily running at night with their lights on, visible to everyone except the ICCS. During my July visit the NVA was probing further to the south and east to re-occupy the jungle areas of the famous War Zone D, north of Saigon. The district town of Phu Giao was unsuccessfully attacked but, by the end of 1973, the direct route from Saigon to the Central Highlands through Phuoc Long and Quang Duc provinces had been cut. Part of this road (Route 14) runs so close to the Cambodian border that the NVA required it for its own supply purposes to Region III. The 'in place' provisions of the cease-fire agreement were, as intended, being completely disregarded.[48]

But a really dangerous threat to Saigon and the Mekong Delta, from which the GVN drew most of its manpower and economic resources, could not be rapidly developed unless the government of Marshal Lon Nol in Phnom Penh could be overthrown. The opportunity was there because the invasion of 1972 had compelled ARVN forces to withdraw from Cambodia into South Vietnam and the Ceasefire Agreement, enforced on the GVN in effect by the American Congress, prevented them from returning. Because a simultaneous ceasefire in Cambodia had not been achieved and because there was no supervision at all by the ICCS of Article 20, which required the withdrawal of all foreign troops from Cambodia, Hanoi had gained a free hand in that country. The situation was very different from 1970, when the NVA could make no headway in the main populated areas because of almost universal support for the new government, assisted as it was by the American incursion of 1970 and by later South Vietnamese operations east of the Mekong. The first flush of enthusiasm in Cambodia, which had boosted the Army from 30,000 to over 200,000 had worn off. Although some units in the Cambodian Army fought courageously with little training, there was behind them little organization and a barely consistent war strategy. With Marshal Lon Nol reduced by illness and with a poor and erratic command structure, the situation had steadily deteriorated. Hanoi had wisely concentrated through 1971 and 1972 less on military operations than on building up the strength of the Khmer Communists (KC) and its own influence over the various factions, few of which supported Prince Sihanouk; most of them had, after all, been attempting to overthrow him for years. Only his support by China is now giving him any standing in the conflict and has enabled him to act as a spokesman. As a result of the KC build-up and the injection of cohesion into their operations by Hanoi, the war in Cambodia flared up again after the ceasefire and a direct threat to Phnom Penh was developed.

Initially the KC, using sensible guerrilla strategy, concentrated on cutting the radial road and river communications to the capital, notably Route 5 to the 'rice basket' of Battambang, Route 4 to the port of Kampong Som (formerly Sihanoukville) and the international waterway of the Mekong river, on which the vital convoys carrying ammunition and petrol were constantly attacked. The threat to Phnom Penh was at this stage a blockade rather than an assault in the hope that confusion and shortages would collapse the government. An assault was however attempted on the provincial town of Takeo, 30 miles south of the capital, to tighten the siege but the town was just held with the help of American air-power. But all this was too slow for Hanoi in the attainment of its three immediate objectives. Firstly, with the cereal shortage in North Vietnam, the last thing Hanoi wanted was to have to transport rice down the Ho Chi Minh trail to its divisions and the population under their control in eastern Cambodia which, as a result of the war and exodus of refugees to Phnom Penh, was only partly cultivated and was no longer a source of supply. Hanoi wanted not only the rice from Battambang in the west but also early control of the rest of Cambodia in time for the 1973 planting season, otherwise rice supplies in 1974 were going to be a major problem. Secondly, Hanoi wanted to re-open Kampong Som as a supply port in the extreme south. Finally the NVA, because the Vietcong could no longer pose such a threat through insurgency, wanted to be able to threaten the comparatively secure Delta (Region IV) and so destroy any chance which the South might have of recovering economically after the ceasefire.

I am fairly convinced that, for these reasons, the North Vietnamese advisers (about 2–3,000) with the KC forces brought pressure to bear on them to change their strategy in May and to concentrate their forces for an all-out offensive against Phnom Penh. Except for these advisers and a few sapper squads, Hanoi did not commit the NVA which was required to hold their positions in South Vietnam or along the border. They could not be spared nor could more than limited supplies be diverted to the KC. That Hanoi was in a hurry in 1973 is the only reason which explains such a conventional assault on Phnom Penh while American air power was still available. Under great pressure from Congress to withdraw it, President Nixon had reached a compromise agreement that it would remain until 15 August. Fortunately also for Cambodia (now the Khmer Republic) the structure of its forces and their command had been reorganized over the previous few months to give far better cohesion and control. Their artillery strength was increased together with additional aircraft, especially transports for supply purposes to the many isolated government garrisons throughout the country. Two months' supply of rice, petrol and ammunition was built up within the city. The rice was particularly important because of the KC tactic of driving out the rural population as refugees into the city. Thirty-six villages just south of Phnom Penh were intentionally burnt down by the KC to intensify this problem for the defenders. But, in spite of this and the gloomy reporting, the city held out and the assault, which was relentlessly maintained for several weeks, faded out.

When I visited the Vietnamese province of Chau Duc, on the Cambodian border along the Mekong river, in early August, I lunched with the province chief and several of the Lower House delegates from the province. All the Vietnamese present thought Phnom Penh would fall after the bombing halt if not before. Only one delegate, himself a Cambodian representing the many Khmers in the province, and myself thought it would not. One interesting fact to emerge, which substantiated the importance of rice to the NVA, was that four hundred Cambodian refugees had recently fled into this province of South Vietnam to get away from fighting between the NVA (1 Division) and the KC over control of territory and rice supplies. Reports of such fighting were repeated elsewhere along the frontier and became fairly common later in 1973. When I made the error of giving a brief interview to the London *Times* correspondent, I mentioned these refugees and the reason for their flight. While the rest of the interview was correctly published, the reason for their flight was given as: 'They were believed to be fleeing from the extremely heavy American bombing which hit the border area in the final few days before its stopping yesterday.' They had fled long before that anyway and the fighting between the NVA and KC was not mentioned in the report. This minor example typifies the hazards of press interviews, and their subsequent reporting, on Vietnam and is about par for the course.

The American bombing in Cambodia in 1973, though heavy with B52s and F111s, was extremely accurate. All populated areas, even villages known to be evacuated in the line of the KC attack, were avoided. The Air Force had by this time become a sharp surgical instrument capable, through smart bombs and other technical aids, of hitting a billiard table. Nevertheless there were still accidents. One B52 in a flight of three, because the offset from the marking beacon had not been fed into its computer, hit the beacon itself which was in the town of Neak Leung. Human error in war, as in peace, is still the major cause of the most ghastly tragedies. There is no excuse, but such failures should not detract either from the present technical efficiency of an Air Force as an instrument of war or from the intense efforts made to avoid civilian casualties at the risk of aircrews.

When I visited Phnom Penh over the weekend before the bombing halt the first signs that the assault was running out of steam were apparent, although there were many who thought that the KC forces were only reforming to renew their attack after the bombing halt. But, in fact, they were pulling back after taking heavy casualties both in the fighting and from the extremely accurate bombing. They were also short of supplies and the monsoon was making re-supply from NVA depots on the Ho Chi Minh trail very difficult. When I discussed the situation with Marshal Lon Nol I told him that I looked forward to seeing him again on my next visit in 1974. A further quick visit over the week-end following the bombing halt reinforced my view that Phnom Penh would hold but I must admit that I did not expect Kampong Cham, which was the next target of attack, to be successfully held, as it was, thanks to valiant re-supply runs up the Mekong by the Khmer Navy.

As promised, I visited Marshal Lon Nol again in February, 1974. The KC, meanwhile, had done a barter deal with the NVA whereby they were re-supplied with about 900 tons of munitions in return for rice. As a result of this the KC attack on Phnom Penh was renewed in the dry season late in 1973. Routes 4 and 5 were both cut but the main supply route up the Mekong river was, surprisingly, not interdicted. This time the KC put in almost all the forces they could raise, probably over eighty battalions, although many of these numbered less than 300. Yet again the assault failed. (I have a sneaking suspicion, because of the very limited NVA assistance given to the KC in 1974, that Hanoi has given up hope of a quick result in Cambodia in order to concentrate on the main target of South Vietnam, and that Hanoi may not be too concerned by the KC failure, because this will enable the North Vietnamese, if there is an eventual take-over, to claim the leadership and to establish their hegemony over Indochina without fear of any successful regional rivals — compare the defeat of the VC in the 1968 Tet offensive.) One effect of the concentration of KC forces around Phnom Penh was that many of the government enclaves elsewhere in the country were able to extend their perimeters by a considerable distance and thousands of people returned to government control. There was much evidence that KC treatment of the rural population had been brutal and this factor may well affect the result, particularly if the government forces are able to push out from Phnom Penh along the routes of communication.

One aspect of this assault was the KC shelling, with captured 105mm guns, of refugee settlements in the southern part of the city. Hundreds were killed and many more wounded. Of course at the time of the shelling there was some panic but as soon as it ceased calm was quickly restored. Although the number of casualties from the shelling was fast approaching that caused by the American bombing of Hanoi at the end of 1972, not one word of condemnation appeared in the American press and the silence of those politicians, who normally get considerable political mileage out of refugees, was deafening.

It became very clear to me on this last visit that the government of Marshal Lon Nol represented the nationalist cause in Cambodia. It stood for independence and eventual neutrality whereas the KC stood for 'limited sovereignty' and alignment with North Vietnam. As between these two there is little chance of reconcilation and the puppetry of Sihanouk has become irrelevant. If ever restored, to give an air of traditional legitimacy to a take-over, he would not last, as he himself admits, for more than a year or two. Once again, the point is that under the present government the people have the prospect of a choice and of determining their own future whereas under the KC they have none.

The prospects for a ceasefire in Laos were better for the simple reason that the NVA had already gained most of its objectives. The Ho Chi Minh trail was absolutely secure and with a ceasefire would become a freeway. The Lao government was hamstrung and could do little more than garrison its major towns along the Mekong, any of which could be taken by the North at any time if it so wished. But with 70,000 NVA troops firmly entrenched in the country there was no hurry, because South Vietnam was still the issue and the rest of Laos, except for the provinces of Phong Saly through which the Chinese have been building two military roads to the northern Thai border, would fall like a domino at any time. Legal camouflage was given to this by the final agreement to establish a 'troika' government in Vientiane, which allowed the stationing of Pathet Lao troops in the capital. Laos could be taken over whenever it suited North Vietnam to achieve its final objective of an Indochina Federation. The status of 'limited sovereignty' was established in fact if not in form and the non-communist Lao forces, including the gallant Meo tribesmen who had fought so valiantly and successfully under General Vang Pao against the invaders for years, had been deserted. I cannot forget the General's remark, during the bloody battle to hold Long Cheng in 1972, when he was needled by an American reporter on his dependence on American aid. The General, whose forces had been mercilessly pounded by Russian 130mm guns, replied venomously: 'Give both sides rocks, we win!'

There was one issue on which Hanoi could not go back nor prevaricate and that was the release of American POWs. Except for the odd stutter in the arrangements with regard to those held by the Vietcong or by the Pathet Lao, they were all released in accordance with the terms of the agreement. I had half thought that, after the biggest blackmail operation in history, Hanoi might fear some repercussions from its treatment of the POWs and from its failure to account for some who were known to be captured but subsequently murdered. But if they are anything, communists are superb judges of human psychology. When the fate of a well-defined group of men is at stake, with the prospect of remaining as prisoners through a never-ending war, emotions can be brought to boiling point. The issue certainly brought out the best in some of American society. I well remember appearing on television with one wife who refused to allow the fate of her husband to be used to influence American policy in any way. As she put it, neither she nor her husband, if he was still alive, could have lived with it. But the issue also turned up some of the nastiest specimens yet to masquerade as human beings who did everything to exploit the feelings of the families concerned for political purposes. But, when the POWs were returned, the harshness and cruelty of their treatment, while it made absorbing reading for a short time, evoked no emotional response and certainly not one of condemnation. The President's late attempt, in the second round of ceasefire negotiations in June, 1973, to insist on accountability for the missing made little or no impression on American public opinion.

When on 15 December, 1973, an American party from the Joint Casualty Resolution Centre (responsible for finding the bodies of those missing in action) was investigating a former crash site, previously arranged with the NVA and VC delegations, it was intentionally ambushed by the VC. The three helicopters were all correctly marked, as were the American personnel with orange armbands. They were also unarmed. Captain Richard Rees, although holding his hands up, was cold-bloodedly murdered and others were wounded. The incident evoked no editorial comment. Although the *Washington Post* reported it on the front page, the *New York Times*, as one American bitingly remarked to me, 'put it among the truss ads'. At least Senator Fulbright inquired into it, but made no fuss. Accountability, like most of the rest of the agreement, is now a dead letter.

The point was, which the communists seemed to understand very well, that live American prisoners in their hands were a powerful weapon of blackmail to be fully exploited. Once released they and their missing comrades, presumed dead, would in the course of events be quickly forgotten. The POWs would leave only one lasting mark. No one in the United States would want to risk the same experience again.

The prisoner situation on the South Vietnamese side was much worse. 26,508 North Vietnamese and Vietcong POWs were released by the GVN during the sixty-day period after the ceasefire. This represented the total held except for 238, who preferred to stay in the South and threatened mass suicide if they were returned to the North, and an additional three, who were too sick to move at the time but whom the South offered to return as soon as they were fit and as soon as the North requested their release. In return the South Vietnamese only got back 4,608 POWs and, although the communists admitted that they were still detaining 410 because of the defection of the 238 North Vietnamese POWs, GVN records showed 31,818 South Vietnamese military personnel captured by the communists so that over 25,000 are still unaccounted for.

On the civilian side the GVN offered to hand over 5,081 of the hard-core communists not releasable in South Vietnam and, as an earnest of this, handed over a first instalment of 1,250. In return the original figure offered by the North Vietnamese was 140. When the GVN remonstrated, this figure was raised to 200, then to 400, then to 429, and finally to 637, whereas the GVN list of South Vietnamese civilians captured by the communists since 1959 totalled 67,501. Over 66,000 South Vietnamese civilian prisoners have just disappeared and not even Amnesty International shows the slightest concern.

The continuation of the war after the ceasefire and the dispute over Vietnamese POWs did not give much hope for a political solution which was the task of the National Council for Reconciliation and Concord. The North Vietnamese and PRG were eager to turn this Council into a form of coalition government and wanted it established in Saigon with branches at provincial level. But this was not provided for in the agreement and they had to be content with meetings in Paris which made little or no progress. President Thieu immediately offered democratic elections under international supervision with complete freedom for communist candidates to stand. But, of course, this offer was rejected as a 'trick', because it was doubtful whether a communist candidate anywhere would secure even 10 per cent of the votes and the communists knew it. They were only prepared to accept elections under the communist system whereby 12 communist candidates are nominated in a constituency and the voters are allowed to choose ten (as in North Vietnam, see Chapter II).

There have been, however, three sanctions operating on Hanoi which did not stem from the agreement. Not one of the three super powers wanted a further flare-up of the war which might damage their new delicate relationships established by the summit meetings of 1972. The Russians had needed 26 million tons of American wheat in that year and might require more in the future. They also needed American technical know-how to help develop their vast natural resources. At the same time, strategically, they wanted at least an apparent *détente* on their European front so that they could pursue their containment of China on the eastern front. China, isolated by this, required to mend her relations with the United States to offset the Russian threat. Although nothing has been said, nor written, it has been assumed that both Russia and China were prepared, as part of their deal with the United States, to restrain Hanoi and to restrict the supply of heavy weapons which North Vietnam would require for the renewal of a sustained general offensive.

The second obvious sanction was the threat of retaliatory bombing by the United States Air Force. That this threat remained was implied by President Nixon in March, 1973, when, in referring to the infiltration of reinforcements and supplies down the Ho Chi Minh trail, he said: 'We have informed North Vietnam about our concern . . . and it has been expressed to other interested parties . . . I would only suggest that in the light of my actions over the last four years . . . North Vietnam should not lightly disregard such expressions of concern.' Weight was added to this message by the use of the Air Force in Cambodia, by three retaliatory raids in Laos, by suspending the removal of the mines and talks on American aid, and by the renewal of American reconnaissance flights over the

North. Although moves in Congress to restrict the President's freedom of action and the Watergate affair have since steadily reduced the credibility of this sanction, the reaction of the President to any future military move by Hanoi, such as a fresh conventional invasion, was still unpredictable. While Richard Nixon remained President Hanoi could never be sure, and made a very considerable effort during 1973 to restore its air defences in the North and down the trail, including the introduction of SAM 3 missiles. There was, however, no indication that Russia was yet prepared to give Hanoi any SAM 6s, as in the case of Egypt, which lent some weight to the validity of the first sanction.

I do not believe that the loss of possible American aid for reconstruction in the North is a sanction. Hanoi did not want it (there were other sources) and knew that it would not get it anyway. Congress, already sour on aid programmes, was unlikely to appropriate it and certainly not in the circumstances which Hanoi foresaw and intended after the ceasefire. Moreover, Hanoi was in no position to absorb it, even at the beginning of 1974, although much lip service was being paid to economic reconstruction. Crates of machinery and other equipment from communist countries and Sweden were left rotting on the roadside between Haiphong and Hanoi. The limited management effort was still concerned with the war. The whole point of including aid as a provision of the ceasefire agreement had been to represent it as an American offer of indemnity and therefore an admission of guilt.

The greatest immediate sanction, however, was the inability of the NVA to renew the offensive or to take on ARVN in conventional battle. The failure and losses of the invasion and the subsequent land-grabbing operations in October, 1972, and February, 1973, had proved the success of Vietnamization. Although, as the defender, the weakness of the South Vietnamese strategic position remained, owing to the shape of its territory and the continual threat to its western border flank through the in-place ceasefire, ARVN units were immeasurably stronger on the ground than the corresponding NVA units. This fact went unrecognized by all the purveyors of gloom, one of whom reported at the time of the ceasefire that 'the crack NVA 7 Division was poised for an attack on Saigon', whereas this division was then down to 1,750 demoralized men and could not even have taken a district town. Hanoi had no intention of committing it or others like it to annihilation. The need to preserve these main force units in existence, as well as in place, was a major factor at the root of the whole Ceasefire Agreement and the main restraint on any large-scale activity in the year after the ceasefire.

Very roughly such activity during 1973 was running at a little more than half the 1971 rate (i.e. before the 1972 invasion). The estimated figures for those killed in action (which should be noted by the Nobel Peace Prize Committee) in the year between the date of the ceasefire, 28 January, 1973, and 27 January, 1974, were NVA/VC 45,057 as compared with 112,496 in 1971, and RVNAF 12,778 as compared with 14,647 in 1971. The two main reasons why South Vietnam's casualties were disproportionally higher were that the fire-power in support of the South Vietnamese forces was greatly reduced and secondly that, in its place, they had to use man-power to recapture outposts and villages in order to rectify the ceasefire-in-place situation. It has been estimated that, at the current scale of activity and at a time when the utmost economy was essential, the South Vietnamese forces were using, as compared with any previous period when they had an unlimited American back-up, about one-fifth of the ammunition and one-tenth of the gasoline. Not only are the South Vietnamese restricted under the agreement to a one-for-one replacement whereas the NVA is not but, in view of the need to reduce the cost of military assistance from the United States, they have had to economize drastically and to meet the gap with lives.

In spite of rumours and various reports (including one in the London *Times* of 30 October, 1973) and in spite of Hanoi's military build-up, there was no sign that Hanoi was yet ready to risk politically or psychologically another general offensive in the South so soon after the previous one had been defeated. On the contrary, from captured documents it appeared that Hanoi was prepared to take a longer term view and to seek her goal initially through military pressure rather than by direct military action. Nevertheless, a general offensive remains a future option if all else fails and is a constant worry to the GVN. It could yet prove to be the greatest test of American determination to maintain world peace. It was quite clear early in 1974 that the pace of activity, although at a lower level than in previous years, was being dictated by Hanoi which had not given up its purpose of taking over the South by force. There was no prospect of reconciliation and the 'violent struggle' would go on. In Indochina, as elsewhere in the world, peace is not at hand.

CHAPTER IX

SOFT OPTIONS

The first soft option open to the United States is, as already stated, to think that the Vietnam war is over, that this tragic episode in United States history can be regarded as closed and that there are no residual commitments.

The rhetoric on the mistakes and might-have-beens of the past, to which I have contributed not on American policy and intentions but on the earlier strategy and conduct of the war, will go on and some people will still be seeking to learn the lessons derived from the original American involvement, from the course and nature of the war, its strategy and tactics. As likely as not the wrong lessons will be learnt rather than the right ones; for example, I doubt whether the U.S. Army will ever learn that in this type of war helicopters only gave them flexibility (in deployment of forces) and some fire-power but not mobility on the ground. Mobility could only be achieved by the ability to range on foot over any terrain with the aim, not just of engaging the enemy in battle but of disrupting his whole logistic system in some depth, thereby reducing his mobility and putting him on the defensive. Because of this freedom of movement both the Vietcong in the early stages of the war and later the NVA retained the initiative throughout (except for a year or so after the Cambodian operation in 1970) in dictating the scale of activity and the timing of offensives. The United States was always reacting and was constantly forced to respond by escalation. The moment that this initiative looked like passing to the GVN and the United States after the defeat of the 1972 offensive, Hanoi, because its hitherto secure rear bases[49] and its mobility were threatened, negotiated an agreement not to end the war but to restore its offensive mobility and therefore its ability to dictate the future pace of the war.

But the past is now really a matter for the more objective historians of the 1980s, if they then exist, but it is interesting to note that much of the dissenting rhetoric was based on events before 1969 and was more muted when the American withdrawal of troops became an irreversible policy and the draft to Vietnam ceased. By that time dissent had done its work and did not have to take into account any of the subsequent events such as the 1972 invasion, the ceasefire negotiations, and the subsequent violations of the ceasefire in 1973, which invalidated many of its previous theories on the war as expounded in the late 1960s.

Regrettably the war is not over, as it might have been if the American will at the end of 1972 had been as high as it was even two or three years previously. Nor is the American involvement yet over. The vital lessons for the future have to be drawn therefore from the situation as it is now in 1974 rather than from the decisions or mistakes of the past on which history can be left to pass judgement.

If I am correct in suggesting that it is not Hanoi's immediate intention over the next year or two to renew an all-out general offensive but to keep this as a long-term option, then Hanoi has no alternative but to continue the type and scale of military pressure that was maintained during the first year of the ceasefire. There are two main reasons for this, the first being that there is no effective political alternative within South Vietnam open to Hanoi or the PRG (they have repeatedly rejected the offer of internationally supervised elections) without the maintenance of such pressure, and the second being that, having sent so many reinforcements and supplies down the trail into South Vietnam, Hanoi cannot allow them to sit and rot.

It is estimated that the NVA's combat strength within South Vietnam was increased in the first year of the ceasefire (in violation of the agreement) by upwards of 20,000 men to about 200,000 in spite of the fact that several divisions were withdrawn across the border into Cambodia, Laos and North Vietnam. These of course could all be redeployed within South Vietnam, as a result of the improved road and rail networks, within a matter of days rather than weeks. It is that redeployment which would herald a possible general offensive. The 200,000 are enough to maintain the military pressure at selected points along South Vietnam's very long borders, particularly when their weaponry is taken into account. Over the first year of the ceasefire the number of 122mm and 130mm guns had been increased from under 100 to over 350 and the tanks from about 100 to over 400 — again in violation of the agreement. The number of AA guns had been increased by 1,000 and, as already stated, sixteen SAM 2s had been installed round Khe Sanh with its brand new airstrip capable of taking MIG 21s.

The policy of restoring the military threat and maintaining military pressure on South Vietnam in 1973 had achieved its main purposes: to prevent RVNAF demobilization, although there was a run-down of about 45,000 in the overall total of South Vietnam's forces instead of the desirable 100,000, thereby keeping the government wages bill very high; to disrupt the South's economy and to frighten off foreign investment; and to keep the cost of American aid at a level which may prove to be unacceptable to those who thought the war was over and who are in any case reluctant to provide further military and economic assistance. By keeping up the military pressure through 1974–75 these three purposes will be maintained, and will put the NVA in a position which will enable it to exploit militarily any favourable opportunity, arising from either the internal economic situation in South Vietnam or the general world and American domestic situation, which might affect future American support for South Vietnam. Such opportunism might be limited to an objective which would be well above the GVN's tolerance level militarily, politically and psychologically, but still be just below the tolerance level of the United States. There are various possible such targets. If such an attack was timed to coincide with demonstrations in Saigon arising out of very high prices and very low salaries, which in turn would affect the morale of the GVN's forces, the military pressure would then have succeeded in creating a dangerous political pressure both in South Vietnam and in the United States. The soft option for the United States would be to pretend that Hanoi had not actually torn up the agreement in their face and to renew talks at the Dr. Kissinger and Le Duc Tho level, which would avoid any decision on an American response, allow the NVA to retain what it had captured and destroy any remaining South Vietnamese faith in the reliability of its ally.

Even without such a scenario South Vietnam's economic problems throughout the next year or two will be severe enough. Inflation in 1973 was about 65 per cent and real wages in 1974 were about one-third of the 1964 level (an object lesson for other countries, including the United Kingdom). Although the 1973 rice crop was good, prospects for 1974 were not bright because, with American aid in any case reduced, the purchasing power of the dollar had declined, world commodity prices had increased and, as everywhere else, the energy crisis had hit. The price of gasoline alone had risen by ten times in two years which affected tractors, water pumps, fishing vessels and transport, all of which are vital to maintaining and increasing agricultural production. This, coupled with the high price and short supply of fertilizer, would affect the production of second annual crops of miracle rice (until the newest strains are introduced, which do not require so much fertilizer). There was also considerable unemployment in the cities and at the beginning of 1974 I heard the words malnutrition and starvation used for the very first time. Although exports had increased there was a gaping balance of trade deficit which could only be met by outside aid.

Fortunately the Vietnamese are a resilient people and extremely hard working. They were also paying their taxes, and revenue in January, 1974, had risen by 50 per cent over the year before. While, more than most people, they can stand a high degree of inflation they cannot however stand simultaneous stagnation. A remarkable job had been done in returning refugees to the southern part of Quang Tri and in resettling the remainder in provinces north and north-east of Saigon, where plenty of land is available, so that they could become productive again. Travelling round the country in early 1974 I have never been so impressed by the intensity of the cultivation; every little plot was being exploited even along the top of the walls of the citadel at Hue, and the quality of production was an inspiration to an amateur vegetable gardener like myself. There was also great austerity. Virtually all sugar and tobacco imports had been given up and bicycles were rapidly replacing Hondas (the import of which have, incidentally, been banned for over five years). The country was in effect trying to get back to a subsistence economy and off a market economy which depended on too great an input of outside resources, such as fertilizer, but this meant that the gross national product would inevitably fall because annual yields would be lower. With the great fall in domestic employment resulting from the American withdrawal and with the population continuing to rise at over 600,000 a year (3 per cent), the burden was becoming very heavy. The need for continuation of American military assistance to meet the military pressure and of economic aid to meet the new economic situation was greater than ever.

There was a widespread belief that, during the years of American involvement, the South Vietnamese had been able to live high off the hog and that, after the ceasefire, imports supported by aid would have to return to 'normal'. Between 1963 and 1973, however, imports increased only at an annual average rate of 7·8 per cent which would be quite normal for a developing country.[50] It is slightly higher than Thailand and Indonesia but well below South Korea, Malaysia and Taiwan, without taking into account South Vietnam's additional war burden at all. Moreover, the import figures have been heavily weighted towards capital goods and raw materials rather than consumer goods by about two-thirds to one-third, although the latter includes food. If there had been peace and if South Vietnam's agricultural and light industry potential had been developed, the import rate would almost certainly have increased by at least this rate through the normal institutional and commercial channels of aid, which are at present denied to it by the war. If sufficient security could be maintained by containment of the NVA and if the present import gap was met by American aid, an economic take-off could still be achieved over the next five years even without the miracle of an oil strike. The prospect of oil is the one bright spot on the horizon, in which most of the major oil companies are interested, and drilling was expected to start in the late summer of 1974.

But the maintenance of security was dependent on continued American military assistance. Yet again few people realized that throughout 1973 this was running well below the permitted level under the ceasefire agreement of a one-for-one replacement. Ammunition stocks had been allowed to drop by over 25 per cent. Not one single helicopter or fixed wing aircraft, except for four F5s,[51] had been replaced and it was the same across the board. The American policy was to provide only the minimum necessary in relation to the scale of activity generated by NVA attacks on GVN towns, villages and outposts and the GVN's response to these.

It was no consolation to South Vietnam that the North required (and was obtaining) equivalent aid from Russia and China and that the North's economy was in a worse state, requiring massive imports of grain and equipment. Even if the management capacity could be re-directed from the war to the economy, it was estimated (by Hanoi's own official spokesman) that it would take 2–3 years to get back to the 1964 level of production. But this prospect is doubtful because, in accordance with Marxist doctrine, the emphasis was being put on heavy industry instead of first on improving the essential agricultural and light industry base, which cannot in any case be greatly expanded under a collectivized system.

It is of course quite impossible to evaluate comparative costs, as between continuing Russian military aid to the North and American to the South, for the simple reason that American aid is accounted at full production costs on the high-priced dollar terms at which the equipment is purchased by the Government from industry, whereas Russia is able to give away surplus equipment no longer required by the Soviet Army. Russia after all has a military industrial complex that is capable of servicing 150 Russian divisions and several satellite armies as well, whereas the equivalent United States' military industrial complex is comparatively peanuts, having to service only thirteen Army and three Marine divisions. With thousands of new tanks, for example, coming off the Russian assembly lines annually, the costs of releasing older, but still very effective, models to client states like North Vietnam is negligible.

But none of these considerations mean anything to those people who would prefer that South Vietnam does not weather its economic crisis, and there have been vigorous attempts to reduce, or even cut off, all American military and economic aid. This is yet another soft option. The arguments produced in favour of such a cut-off have been based mainly on moral grounds which depend in turn on some of the subjects dealt with in the first three chapters of this book. The main theme yet again was the '200,000 political prisoners'. I have had the privilege of meeting and knowing well the last two American ambassadors to South Vietnam, Ellsworth Bunker and Graham Martin, men of great honour and of the highest integrity in the best American tradition. They both utilized the considerable resources of their embassy to determine the truth or falsehood of this allegation. Ambassador Martin reached this conclusion early in February, 1974: 'I can state with complete conviction that the total prison population within the Republic of Vietnam, including all prisoners from the smallest village detention facility to the largest central prison does not exceed 35,000.' While not being able to state (as I cannot) that there were no political prisoners, however defined,[52] he could state 'with absolute accuracy' that 'in almost seven months of conversations with opponents of this (Thieu's) Government, with independent journalists, with representatives of great humanitarian organizations of both my own country and of other countries of the world I have yet to be given the name of a prisoner who is incarcerated solely for his opposition to the present government of Vietnam. I find that to be an astounding fact and one which bears true witness to the efficacy of the Hanoi propaganda efforts.'

But what, you may say, about Madame Ngo Ba Thanh whose case in this respect was given considerable publicity in the United States? I would like to know what would happen to a lady in the United States who, after a hearing before a Federal high court judge or a Supreme Court judge, accosted him outside the court, beat him with her umbrella, smashed the windscreen of his car and kicked him in the balls. I strongly suspect that she would go to gaol, which is exactly what happened to Madame Ngo in South Vietnam. She was later released, was free to stay and continue her criticism (which she did) or to leave the country if she wished. She is no political threat whatever to President Thieu.

Great care has of course been taken by Hanoi never to vary

the simple propaganda themes. The figure of '200,000 political prisoners' has been consistent in their publications for over ten years. (Goebbels was a master at this sort of repetition but he must be writhing in his grave with envy.) Even those who recognize that 200,000 is a gross fabrication have to yield to the temptation to maintain their own 'credibility' by accepting some lesser number. In this way, from the propaganda platforms which have been made available to it through worldwide communist and left-wing organizations, Hanoi has found no difficulty in absorbing into its fold a large portion of the intellectual and student community driven by a compulsion to ensure that their conforming hemlines are not one millimetre above or below the prevailing fashion. Although the themes are simple there has been the need to manipulate them to achieve the primary objective at any given moment. The greatest barrier to a successful subversive and guerrilla organization is an efficient Police Force and the theme therefore was first used to destroy American support for that force in South Vietnam. It has since been used to reduce or cut off completely all external aid to the GVN, and an intense campaign, deriving from the PRG representatives in Paris and from the Stockholm 'Peace' Conference, was mounted to lobby Congress in the spring of 1974.

The obligation and continuing commitment of the United States is inherent in the Ceasefire Agreement itself. The terms of that agreement were made by the United States with North Vietnam over the South's misgivings and its understanding of Hanoi's intentions. President Thieu had no alternative but to accept these terms, but on the understanding that they would be enforced and that the one-for-one replacement of military equipment and American economic aid, as allowed under the agreement, would continue. The United States did not enforce the agreement and this therefore has increased rather than reduced their obligation on the second count. The obligation may not be legally binding but morally it is absolute. If these 'moral' propaganda themes are used to justify the cutting off of aid, then Solzhenitsyn's contempt for western double standards and selective outrage will prove to be well founded. The United States will indeed be making a 'moral grimace' towards a softer opposition in order to excuse a greater moral cowardice towards a tougher one.

There is an even softer option in respect of aid which is almost too distasteful to report. It has been proposed that American obligations should be met merely by giving 'humanitarian' aid to the children, the widows, the orphans, the war victims and the refugees, and to purchase the acquiescence of the voluntary humanitarian organizations by channelling this aid through them, thereby muzzling any revulsion at such a cynical, hypocritical and callous perversion of the word 'humanitarian' by using these innocent victims as pawns in a scheme to ensure that there could not possibly be any hope of a satisfactory environment for their future (nor one in which humanitarian organizations would be allowed to operate). Not many people realize that, whereas 71 per cent of South Vietnam's budget in 1970 was spent on defence and only 9 per cent on health and social welfare, the corresponding figures for 1974 were 52 per cent and 19 per cent. It is a country which, through its past village and family social systems and now its state system, has had a remarkably good comparative record in assisting the handicapped.

In the bitter debate and confused thought of today it has been tempting to take yet another soft option and to sweep the unpleasant consequences under the rug. For example, the rejection of the domino theory is comforting to some because it salves their conscience, or suits their political view, while to others it enables them to follow the current fashion. The theory is never mentioned in the press unless preceded by the usual pejoratives of 'discredited' or 'out-dated'. It certainly cannot be out-dated because it has not yet been tested and, with regard to discrediting, I rather like President Johnson's laconic comment in his memoires: 'I realize that some Americans believe that they have, through talking with one another, repealed the domino theory.' The theory has been endorsed by the last four American Presidents and their senior advisers and supporters. As late as September, 1968, when he was running for the Presidency, Vice-President Humphrey felt constrained to say: 'I sincerely believe that our stand in Vietnam has surely been of some significant help to stability and security in that part of the world. And that is vital to our national interest, because if all Asia were to go communist, and fall prey to aggression, or at least all of Southeast Asia, the power balance in this world would be thrown out of kilter completely, and there's no way of predicting what the cost would be to this country in terms of its own defense.'

This quite sensibly carries the consequences of the domino theory well beyond the immediate confines of South East Asia, but even in that area no Asian has yet repealed the domino theory and the answer is to ask the dominoes. As long ago as 1961 Tunku Abdul Rahman, the first Prime Minister and architect of independent Malaya (and later Malaysia), asked me to go to Vietnam 'to help hold my front line'. In October, 1967, Mr. Lee Kuan Yew, the socialist Prime Minister of Singapore, said: 'Nothing would be more disastrous than to see South Vietnam just rot away and become absorbed into the communist group . . . if people start believing that non-communist Asia will be lost eventually to communist Asia, then everybody will make his decisions accordingly.' He has made many similar pronouncements since.

More revealing is the following statement: 'The communisation of Cambodia would be the prelude to the communisation of all South East Asia and, finally, (although in the longer run) of Asia. Thus it is permitted to hope that, to defend its world interests (and indeed not for our sake), the United States will not disentangle itself too quickly from our area—in any case not before having established a more coherent policy which will enable our population to face the Communist drive with some chance of success.' That surely must have come from some pillar of the non-communist establishment such as Marshal Lon Nol, but it did not. It was written by Sihanouk in early 1970 when he was still ruler of Cambodia and free to say what he liked and before he adopted his present puppet role.

Of course the domino theory can be shot down if it is accepted too literally and mechanically that neighbour knocks down neighbour and that the mechanical force has to be exactly the same as that applied in Vietnam. But in its general sense the theory is still valid if it is thought of in terms of erosion, re-alignment and adjustment as part of the initial falling process.

This is already apparent both in Thailand and Malaysia, because some people think that South Vietnam is about to fall, and in both countries the armed communist insurgent forces are slowly expanding to exploit any future opportunity.[53] But more significant was a question which I put to a friend of mine in the United States just before the Presidential election in 1972: 'Do the Jews in the United States not realize that, if South Vietnam falls as a result of an American failure, Israel will be the next domino?' I have no doubt that one of the major contributing factors to the 1973 Middle East war was the Arabs' belief that they could blackmail the United States with oil, just as Hanoi had with POWs, and for the same purpose— to weaken their support for their ally. Equally, as a result of the advantages gained by Hanoi from the Ceasefire Agreement, Syria and Egypt appreciated that they had the more reliable ally, and so it proved, as explained in the last chapter. If Americans were complaining of the shortage of gasoline, a few of them may at least have been beginning to realize the cost of soft options. That shortage is only a minor problem compared with what may be to come.

The dissent over the domino theory was carried a great deal further than the attempt to discredit it. Even those who grudgingly accepted it had another soft option to play: 'What does it matter if they all go communist?' It should be noted at once that such people said 'they' and precluded 'we'. In other words they still had a dividing line. But they have not yet thought out where it is, how they will hold it, nor at what risk and at what cost. At least on the present line the United States has been supporting a people who have been prepared to fight and who, if that support continues, are prepared to go on defending for as long as the other side goes on attacking.

The South Vietnamese people have fought on a scale and at a cost which far outweighs any contribution made by the United States and their resilience and stamina have been incomparable. There have been many ignorant critics of their fighting quality. Not one of these critics would have believed in 1968 that over 500,000 American troops could be withdrawn and that South Vietnam would still stand and defeat a massive invasion which few other countries in the world could have

168

withstood even with the support of American air power. The Vietnamese have known all along that they were in for a long war and that their strategy and tactics had to be adjusted accordingly to keep casualties below a tolerance level which, if exceeded, might have affected morale throughout the Army. For example, many positions might have been captured or re-captured by a direct set piece assault with élite troops at a cost to the units concerned of 30–40 per cent casualties. (Why do Americans have such a predilection for Clausewitz's frontal assaults over Liddell Hart's indirect approach?) Such an assault would have sent a shock wave through the Army and every unit would have wondered: 'When are they going to do it to us?' It is exactly the same principle on which RAF Bomber Command operated during the war: that crews could stand a nightly attrition rate below 5 per cent for thirty opera-tions before being relieved (i.e. almost 150 per cent casualties over a period) but that the whole campaign would have come to a grinding halt if the nightly casualties had gone over that. It was an intolerable loss level which defeated the German submarine and bombing (of the United Kingdom) campaigns. The best South Vietnamese generals understood this tolerance level very well, even though their critics in the American media did not. Having seen quite a number of armies over the years I am prepared to state that ARVN is now second only to Israel in this type of modern warfare in the western world.

If South Vietnam were to fall at any time in the future and that army was taken over as part of the army of a united Viet-nam (as the Nationalist army was taken over in China), its strength in the world would be third only to Russia and China. If it started moving there would be nothing in South East Asia to stop it. Its intimidatory effect alone would be enough to crash the dominoes.

One favourite argument of those who consider that the United States have no national interest in Vietnam or South East Asia rests on the proposition that their only really vital interests are the industrialized areas of the world, such as Japan and western Europe. Obviously such a short list might be ex-tended a little but the fallacy of the argument is still self-evident. It is not only industrial power that matters in the strategic context. Excluding geographical strategic locations, which are important enough in themselves, two other factors matter as much if not more than industry—commodities and people. The commodity problem has been brought directly home to the West over oil and it is worth remembering that South East Asia alone produces, amongst other things, about three-quarters of the world's natural rubber and tin. It is also a great trading area and distribution centre, as well as a transit area for many vital commodities (oil and iron ore) for industrial nations like Japan.

The loss of all the dominoes in this way would have just as disastrous an effect on world trade and the monetary system as the energy crisis. I doubt if the West could stand both in the same decade. A further effect (as foreseen by Senator Humphrey when Vice-President) would be the cost of defence. When the people of the United States wake up to the situation, their defence budget could go through the roof. It is now over $90 billions and rising and would probably approach $150 billions (at 1974 prices), since there is always a tendency to over-react in such circumstances. What is worse, not only would the budget be high but, if the United States were then going to regain a credible foreign policy and stand on a new line, greater risks would have to be taken and greater commitments made because credibility would be lower. When the West failed to stand on the Saar, on the Sudetenland, Austria and Czechoslovakia in the late 1930s, it finally stood on Poland where it had no hope of preventing Hitler's invasion or of saving Poland when the invasion came.

The Russians also understand very well that the primary target is people and people's minds (Stalin's 'vast stores of human material'). It is most noticeable that over the last thirty years Russia has not directed her efforts towards industrial areas but towards the countries with the largest populations by backing China against Japan, India against Pakistan, the Arabs against Israel, and even Nigeria against Biafra. American have never been strategically minded in that sense possibly because of their ignorance of the world outside. By a rare chance I happened to catch a quiz programme on American TV in which three competing college teams were answering astonishing questions with computer-like speed and accuracy. They were then shown a picture of some golden pagodas and told these were in the city of Rangoon, the capital of a country bordering Thailand and China. What was the name of the country? There was a stupefying silence. They were completely stumped.[54] And yet there is a large body of American students which claims to know all the answers on South East Asia and exactly what the peoples of that area want. Even Senator Fulbright can write off most of the people of Indochina and Thailand as 'nomadic tribes or uneducated subsistence farmers', thereby implying that they are of no account and not worth any American concern. That is a false argument if only because it reduces the stature and completely denies the basic ideals of the United States. Let me say here that I do not consider that the 47,000 Americans who died in Vietnam and the hundreds of thousands who were wounded fought in vain, if South Vietnam manages to come through, as it still could. Twenty million people will have been saved, the line held, and much direr consequences prevented.

That raises two important reasons why it does matter if 'they all go communist'. The first is that millions would die in a bloodless bath and those who survived would be subjected to the unending misery and tyranny of a totalitarian state. In my article for the *New York Times* (Chapter II) I gave the lowest accepted figure of twenty million deaths in respect of Soviet Russia. That figure has now been corrected by Alexander Solzhenitsyn who has stated that: 'In addition to the toll of the two world wars, we have lost, as a result of civil strife and tumult alone—as a result of internal political and economic "class" extermination alone—sixty-six million people.' Of course we won't see it and will hardly believe it when we hear it. It will probably be excused on the argument that at least the survivors are better off. That is certainly the line that will be taken by western communist parties and fellow travellers[55] and their hangers-on in the intellectual community. This is what Solzhenitsyn calls 'this grim humour of the twentieth century; how can such a discredited and bankrupt doctrine still have so many followers in the west! In our country there are fewest of all left.' But on a totalitarian dictatorship Lenin is a better judge when he wrote in 1916: 'When we get power we will establish a dictatorship of the proletariat . . . dictatorship is the rule of a part of society over the whole of society, and moreover, a rule basing itself directly on force.' Two years later he observed: 'Dictatorship is a serious, heavy and even bloody word', and in 1920 he reminded his opponents: 'The scientific concepts of dictatorship mean neither more nor less than unlimited power resting directly on force, not limited by anything, not restricted by any laws nor any absolute rule. Nothing else but that.' To me there is little to choose between the dictatorship of the left or the dictatorship of the right. They sometimes make good allies when they can share the spoils.[56] I have spent thirty-five years fighting both.

The second reason why it matters derives from the fact already mentioned that the main Soviet target has been not the industrial proletariat but the peoples of large agricultural countries. This is a matter of real concern because it could lead to a situation where perhaps three-quarters of the population of the world, through adopting a Marxist economy, is starving beyond even the capacity of North America to feed it. As I wrote nine years ago: "The so-called 'newly emerging forces' are rapidly in danger of becoming the future starving masses".[57] Agriculture is the one subject above all on which communist theories have dismally failed. Solzhenitsyn, naturally, has plenty to say on this point: 'We shudder after one year of drought . . . and all because we won't admit our blunder over the collective farms. For centuries Russia exported grain, 10–12 million tons a year just before the first world war, and here we are after 55 years of the new order and 40 years of the much vaunted collective farm system, forced to import 20 million tons per year! It's shameful—it really is time we came to our senses. The village, for centuries the mainstay of Russia, has become its chief weakness.' Castro has now joined the ranks of those who lament the loss of the market economy to the Marxist economy: when he admitted that it took many more workers today to carry out the same duties in the island's sugar factories than it did under American owners and that 'the fault is ours because we have not been capable of developing administrative efficiency so that it could at least be equal to that of the capitalists'.

To get round this agricultural weakness some Soviet farmers are now permitted to own small private plots of land and can sell the produce at whatever price they can get. The figures are quite staggering. These private plots are only 3 per cent of the total farm acreage but they produce 63 per cent of Russia's potatoes, 38 per cent of its vegetables, 35 per cent of its milk, 51 per cent of its meat and 20 per cent of its wool. Hanoi of course adopted the collectivized farm system and its people and production suffered accordingly. It is an irony that one effect of the bombing campaign between 1965 and 1968 was to compel Hanoi to allow private plots. These were so successful that they had to be rapidly cancelled because they were completely undermining the doctrinal purity of the regime and wrecking the revolution. It is alarming to think what the American aid bill may be if it has to feed a collectivized world throughout all the areas which according to some are of no national interest to the United States. It is even more alarming to think what might happen if the United States does not feed them.

Finally, there is the softest option of them all: if you surrender, the war will end and the killing will stop. It is seldom put quite as bluntly as that but unlimited concessions are advocated as a means of satisfying the appetite of the other side. As we have seen Hanoi's main purpose in negotiating was to win at the table concessions which had not been won on the battlefield and which would end the war in its favour. There are many who put forward this line in respect of Cambodia. It is a line which has got the world into spectacular trouble because it means that violence and blackmail pay. We have seen it with the POWs, all forms of terrorism, hijacking, oil and, in the United Kingdom, coal miners. Every instance may be a small one and it is tempting to give way but the cumulative effect is cultivating a trend which is softening everyone's will to resist.

I am still glad to say that it was not the option adopted by the United Kingdom in 1940 nor by the United States in December, 1941. Nor is it the option which the United States can afford to adopt now. One excuse sometimes put forward for adopting it is that North Vietnam is going to gain control over Indochina anyway (Ambassador Joseph Kennedy's excuse for Hitler towards the United Kingdom in 1940). I do not agree with that judgement in any case but, even if it should be proved correct, for South Vietnam to fall of its own accord is one story; for it to fall, because the United States took this soft option and cut off aid, would be a very different story.

Let there be no mistake; the choice of any of these options by the United States will be fully understood in the rest of the world and those who have to take future decisions will draw the correct conclusions as to the standing and calibre of the United States within the international community. The consequence of a complete American desertion of its ally will be disastrous. President Nixon put it in these terms: 'All the power in the world lodged in the United States means nothing unless those who depend upon U.S. power to protect them from the possibilities of aggression from other powers, which they themselves would not be able to do, all the power in the world here means nothing unless there is some assurance, some confidence, some trust that the United States will be credible, will be dependable . . .'

Whatever may be the effect of Watergate or its outcome, it does not in any way affect the mandate in the foreign policy field on which the President was overwhelmingly re-elected. Whatever the temptations or excuses, if this final soft option is adopted over Vietnam, it will raise the deadly question: Will the United States in a future crisis adopt this option for themselves and acquiesce in their own strategic surrender?

CHAPTER X

STRATEGIC SURRENDER

When World War III is discussed most people think of it in terms of a nuclear exchange between Russia and China or between Russia and the United States, either of which would drag us all in, but it is quite pointless to think in terms of winning the war by that means. In the present state of over-kill the world would be obliterated; that would be lunacy, and the Russians know it like everyone else. The thesis, therefore, which I wish to propose is that we have been in World War III for the past twenty-five years and that the long-range Soviet goal is to win it without a nuclear exchange. This requires that eventually there should be a strategic surrender by the United States, brought about either politically and psychologically by a loss of will and purpose or politically and militarily by manœuvring the United States into a vulnerable and untenable global situation, or a bit of both.

Since World War II American grand strategy has inevitably been defensive in protection of its own national interests and those of its allies and of what has come to be known as the 'free world in general' or, put more succinctly, the status quo. Russian grand strategy on the other hand has been correspondingly offensive. There has been a tendency on the part of the United States, stemming from previous policies of isolation and protectionism and now from loss of will, to pull back but on the part of Russia, stemming from earlier Tsarist imperialist policies, now justified by a communist expansionist ideology which is politically missionary and economically imperialist, to push forward. The late President Kalinin's remark in 1945 set the tone for what followed: 'Even now, after the greatest victory known to history, we cannot for one minute forget the basic fact that our country remains the one socialist State in the world.' If he were alive today to look at the map, to see the deployment of Russian military and naval power or to count the heads in the United Nations, he would be extremely gratified.

In her expansionist policy Russia has always had the initiative and also the advantage of a consistent policy, which is available to a totalitarian state but not to an open society liable to a constant change of government. Russia has had a variety of instruments to support her policy—the Soviet army, notably in Europe between 1945 and 1948; satellite armies, dependent on Russian supplies and political support such as North Korea, North Vietnam, Egypt and Syria; revolutionary war from Greece to Vietnam; united front tactics as in Italy and France; and trade and aid as in India and elsewhere. More importantly, however, in the use of these instruments Russia has been able to adopt a flexible strategy because at every stage her leaders have learnt the lessons. The first stage was the Cold War. This from the Russian point of view, though perhaps necessary in terms of her domestic situation to create a bogey, proved to be a mistake internationally. It led to NATO, CENTO and SEATO[58] and to the containment of Russia, who found that any direct confrontation automatically united the West behind the United States and alerted Western public opinion to the threat.

The death of Stalin in 1953 ushered in a new period of 'co-existence'. This was designed to meet a situation where the western alliance did not yet look like collapsing of its own accord from within and could not be overthrown by conventional military action or the threat of it. This period has no fixed duration and continues today (with '*détente*' as the new catchword) as the more likely means of achieving either of these possibilities. That peaceful 'co-existence' meant an end to the struggle between the two systems was categorically denied by Mr. Brezhnev at a dinner for Castro in 1972: 'While pressing for the assertion of the principle of peaceful co-existence, we realise that successes in this important matter in no way signify the possibility of weakening the ideological struggle. On the contrary, we should be prepared for an intensification of this struggle and for its becoming an increasingly more acute form of the struggle between the two social systems.' Struggle, in the communist sense and in this context, includes all forms of violence below the level of war between the major powers.

Russia has been learning her lessons from the failures and

successes of this period of 'co-existence' too: Suez in 1956, when the Russians and their bombers fled from Egypt; the Congo in 1960; the missile crisis in Cuba in 1962; the Vietnam war;[59] the Middle East wars of 1956, 1967 and 1973; and, often forgotten by many people, the Malaysian confrontation with Indonesia which led to the fall of Sukarno and the elimination of the Indonesian Communist Party in 1965.[60] Russia found that positive action in all these crises, except to some extent in the Middle East, would have required taking risks at a range beyond her capability at the time.

It must be recognized that Russia's primary military aim, after her experience of Hitler's invasion and others in her past history, has been the security of the Soviet base on both its European and Chinese fronts. This accounted for her immediate post-war intervention policy in eastern Europe to install communist governments through the presence of the Soviet army, for the invasion of Hungary in 1956 and Czechoslovakia in 1968, for her present diplomacy designed to secure recognition of the post-war European boundaries as permanent, and for her forty-four divisions now deployed on the Chinese front. It only partly accounts for the enormous Warsaw Pact conventional superiority over NATO on the key northern and central European fronts of 67 divisions (41 Russian) to NATO's 24, of 20,000 tanks to NATO's 6,000 and of 4,200 aircraft to NATO's 2,064. For defensive purposes this superiority is quite unnecessary because at no time since World War II, even when the United States were the sole possessors of the atomic bomb, has there been any Western military threat to Russia at all. As Solzhenitsyn has written: 'For the next half-century our only genuine military need will be to defend ourselves against China, and it would be better not to go to war with her at all . . . *No one else on earth* (his italics) threatens us, and no one is going to attack us. For peacetime we are armed to excess several times over; we manufacture vast quantities of arms that are constantly having to be exchanged for new ones; and we are training far more manpower than we require who will anyway be past the age for serving by the time the military need arises.' These excessive forces are being used to retain control in eastern Europe, to intimidate Yugoslavia, to extend the Finlandization process to western Europe (as a means of obtaining by political and military pressure friendly and eventually subservient governments) and to place an indefinite burden on the United States for the military support of western Europe.

Even so Russia's conventional forces, while dominant on the continental land mass of Europe and northern Asia, did not make her a global power, but they gave her the secure base from which to become one. Throughout the period of 'co-existence' Russia has been steadily building up her strategic military power both in nuclear weapons and in terms of air and naval mobility. By 1973 Russia had 1,530 intercontinental ballistic missiles (ICBMs) with a further ninety under construction as compared with America's 1,054. Russia also had 628 submarine-launched ballistic missiles (SLMs) with at least 200 under construction as compared with America's 656.[61] While it was thought at the time of the first Strategic Arms Limitation Talks (SALT) that the United States still had a technical superiority in the number of separable warheads (MIRVs), Russia has since achieved a breakthrough in this field and has, in addition, superiority in her anti-ballistic missile (ABM) defence system. By the time this book is read these figures will be out of date, and it can be assumed that Russia, by breaching at least the spirit of the first SALT agreement, will have a nuclear capability equal if not superior to that of the United States, in addition to an overwhelming conventional capability. As Mr. James Schlesinger, the American Secretary of Defense, cautiously put it: 'Now, as the Soviet Union reaches nuclear parity with the United States, deterrence will be strongly reinforced if there is a balance of conventional as well as nuclear forces . . . Thus, a strong conventional capability is more than ever necessary—not because we wish to wage conventional war, but because we do not wish to wage any war.'

The really staggering increase over the last ten years has been in Russia's naval construction to a strength of over 230 major surface ships and 300 attack submarines (now probably underestimated) with more being built, including aircraft carriers presumably for the Mediterranean, Indian Ocean and Persian Gulf. With the Suez Canal being reopened (and cleared by the United States!) in the near future, Russia will be in a position, whether the Arab or Persian Gulf states like it or not, to threaten in a time of crisis both the production of Middle East oil and its supply routes.[62] Russia learnt from Germany that, in strategic terms against the maritime industrial countries of the West, naval forces and, above all, a submarine fleet can be strangulating. But in the naval field Russia learnt further lessons from the nineteenth century and from World War II which taught the West the wrong lessons. The lesson which the West learnt from World War II was that aircraft or missiles can sink battleships. What the West failed to understand was that naval ships can only be sunk if there is a declared war. Russia realized that a navy is visible and that the pressures which can be imposed by a visible naval threat are much greater than those which can be imposed by an invisible air force thousands of miles away. Gunboats are still a most effective instrument of policy.[63] They are also ideal for filling vacuums whether in the Indian Ocean or later in South East Asia and the South China Sea. This was the major reason (the possibility of oil is remote) why China, having ignored them for the whole of this century, suddenly grabbed the Paracel Islands off the Vietnamese coast.

How did the United States face up to the post-war situation? Immediately after the war there was a tendency to believe, particularly with the establishment of the United Nations, that world peace had been restored, and therefore to pull back from any overseas commitments. But the Russian attempt to hold on to Azerbaijan in Iran, contrary to the Yalta agreement between Stalin, Roosevelt and Churchill towards the end of the war, Russian pressure on Turkey to station troops on the Bosphorus and the civil war in Greece soon brought the United States back into the world. There followed the Marshall Plan for the economic recovery of Europe, the Berlin airlift, and the Korean war resulting in the NATO, SEATO and CENTO alliances which established the United States as the leading defender of the West against Russian (or communist) expansion. The outstanding statement of that time was made by President Truman in 1947 when he went down to Congress and said: 'It must be the policy of the United States to support free peoples who are resisting subjugation by armed minorities or outside pressures.' The Truman doctrine was the corner-stone of Western defence for twenty years but was destroyed by the trauma of the Vietnam war. It was replaced by the Nixon doctrine laying down that the United States would give nuclear guarantees to its allies, would meet its treaty commitments (it is astonishing that this had to be stated) and, thirdly, would give aid and military assistance to those who were prepared to be primarily responsible for providing the manpower for their own defence. In effect this repeated the Truman doctrine but, by stressing self-reliance, added a limitation which was not there before. But what will happen to the Nixon doctrine if South Vietnam, Cambodia, Laos and Israel finally fall?

It is interesting to note the complete swing in the self-reliance theme over the last decade. Ten years ago self-reliance was a basic doctrine in the communist attitude to revolutionary movements, whereas the United States were almost prepared to brush their clients aside in their readiness to do it for them. These attitudes have since been almost reversed. A few years ago Egypt leaked with malicious glee how five MIGs with Russian pilots were shot down by the Israelis over the Canal Zone. The Russians played a major part in preparing and running the air defences of Egypt and Syria in 1973. Even North Koreans were flying Syrian MIGs and North Vietnamese were manning SAM sites. China, too, is becoming directly involved with revolutionary movements in Africa. The GI, on the other hand, has become an invisible man. That is a recipe for failure.

A point which I made over four years ago is still valid: 'It has to be accepted that involvement can lead to either success or failure. Non-involvement only leads to failure, possibly a less expensive failure, but a failure none the less. The answer is to keep the options open.'[64]

During the latter part of this period of 'co-existence' we are supposed to have moved into an era of negotiation. No one can complain that there has not been a flurry of dramatic negotiations from summit meetings to desert-hopping exchanges. Unfortunately no one has yet mastered in the art of negotiating with Russia or Russian-supported countries. It is possible that in the nuclear field there will be further agreement at the SALT talks because the costs are becoming astronomical even for a totalitarian state but, in terms of advantage, it is likely that Russia will achieve the better bargain. As an additional bonus she may obtain more wheat, technical know-how and trade credits for which some political price ought to be paid. On the 1972 wheat deal Russia was the sole winner because it helped to create a world economic crisis over food and commodity prices, and the wheat itself was paid for with a devalued dollar and gold bullion, the price of which had meanwhile soared. In the field of conventional forces, through the European Security Conference, an expectation of a mutual reduction of forces has been widely encouraged but, with Russia steadily increasing her conventional capability in Europe, the chance of such a reduction being balanced is remote so that in the end the present disparity may become an even greater disparity.

There are two false attitudes in the West's approach to negotiations. The first is that any agreement, even a bad one, is better than no agreement at all. It is a matter of faith in the West that negotiation and a willingness to compromise and make concessions will solve a conflict and produce a settlement. This, in the face of all the evidence, is simply not true—unless the desire to reach a settlement on both sides is mutual and the concessions are balanced. To communists, as compared with the West, the ending of conflict is not a self-evident or necessarily a desirable goal. Negotiating to them (see Chapter VII) is part of the conflict and is designed to consolidate gains, to bring greater pressure to bear on the weakest element in the opposition or to obtain a respite. The art of 'guerrilla diplomacy' has been inadequately researched and has been understood by only a few,[65] even after the event. For example, how many people understand that the sole communist purpose behind the Laos Agreement of 1962 was to safeguard North Vietnam's use of the Ho Chi Minh trail without which the attack on South Vietnam could not have been pursued? The second false attitude is that somehow peace and violence are divorcible, and that peace can be preserved by allowing a tolerable level of violence to continue. It is certainly not tolerable to those who suffer from it, although it may be to those who are remote, or remove themselves, from it. At some point that violence will spread and the tolerance level will be breached thereby endangering peace. The very fact that there is this tolerance level stems partly from the readiness to accept bad and unenforceable agreements.

There has been yet another swing—in Western attitudes to treaties and agreements. During World War II Russia had occupied the Iranian border province of Azerbaijan but the written agreement made at Yalta was quite specific about the withdrawal of all Allied forces from Iran. Russia attempted to hold on to it and, although it was remote and no American had ever heard of it, Britain and the United States insisted on a Russian withdrawal to comply with the agreement. There would be no such universal condemnation today of breaches of a treaty. The pattern seems to have been set by the Laos Agreement of 1962. The United States are happy to make binding concessions on behalf of their allies and themselves and to ignore subsequent breaches on the part of their adversaries, under the delusion that insistence on strict observance would be provocative and imperil 'peace'.

It is not surprising that negotiations to end wars have not exactly proved successful. There have been two wars between India and Pakistan with no real settlement and, in Indochina, North Vietnam is making a farce of the Ceasefire Agreement. The best example, however, is the Middle East where, in spite of the summit meetings and *détente*, Russia armed and incited the Arab states to have a go—even those like Algeria which in the event did not become directly involved. Within days Russian Antonov transports were pouring fresh supplies into Syria but it was nearly a week before the United States responded to the pleas of Israel. At this stage, with the Egyptians streaming across the Suez Canal, there was no question of a ceasefire, when the Russian side looked as if it was winning. But the moment that the Israeli counter-stroke back across the Suez Canal faced the Egyptians with complete military disaster, even greater than that in 1967, Dr. Kissinger was summoned to Moscow and the Russians demanded, and got, an immediate ceasefire. This would have put the Israeli forces across the canal in an impossible situation, because their safety depended solely on being able to maintain the momentum of their thrust. Standing still their meagre mobile forces were open to envelopment. They had to continue for two days until they had the Egyptian Third Army by its jugular at Suez and their own position was thereby secured. Now, under pressure for a permanent settlement, they will have to make concessions, which will expose their security and risk their survival, in return for a loose American guarantee. There is no certainty of a lasting settlement and, under the threat of a further oil embargo, an American guarantee could prove somewhat flimsy. The Vietnam Ceasefire Agreement and the subsequent reluctance of Congress to continue aid to South Vietnam were an object lesson which all allies of the United States have had to heed.[66] In the Middle East crisis the behaviour of America's European allies may have been 'craven' and 'contemptible', but it should not be surprising if they are now just a little cautious in going along with the United States.

The point to understand is that in Indochina, the Middle East and in Europe Russia has managed to establish for herself and for her allies a can-win can't-lose situation, in which the allies of the United States only have to lose once (and step by step in some cases). The latter are therefore completely dependent on the United States fulfilling their guarantees. The domino theory does not apply only in South East Asia (as explained in the previous chapter). We are all dominoes.

'Co-existence' and negotiations are meaningless words when not matched by deeds and the least provocative description of the situation today is that we are in a period of controlled violence and instability within the illusion of a *détente*, with the status quo liable to constant and turbulent change. It is worth recalling Khrushchev's definition of the status quo, as explained by him to President Kennedy in Vienna nearly fifteen years ago—that the continuing revolutionary process in various countries is the status quo and that anyone who tried to halt this process is not only altering the status quo, but is an aggressor. That definition, if accepted, would make defence against Russian or communist expansion both illegal and immoral, and some people can be persuaded to fall for it.

The Russians have also succeeded in establishing some advantageous ground rules. The first is that communist countries (or socialist as defined by Russia) are off-limits while the rest of the world is a free-for-all. Eastern Europe, North Korea, Cuba and North Vietnam have all established that. Secondly, in a free-for-all a communist party (or a Russian ally) only has to win once. This view was well expressed as part of the Brezhnev doctrine when he said: 'Experience shows us that in the present conditions, the victory of the socialist system in this or that country can be regarded as final and the restoration of capitalism can be regarded as precluded.' In other words neither the ballot box nor revolt can ever throw the communists out. Thirdly, revolutionary parties know that they will be supported (by Russia, China or both) whereas threatened governments and peoples do not know whether they will be supported by the United States.

That is a dangerous situation rendered more so by Russia's understanding of the meaning of power. The simple formula is that manpower + applied resources × will = power, where 'will' is never greater than a factor of one. In all these three ingredients Russia outstrips the United States. Whereas Russia may be cautious, as in the case of the invasion of Czechoslovakia, and her will is less than a factor of one, it is still regrettably higher in most cases than that of the present United States. For example, what would the American will factor be today over Berlin, or for that matter over Israel if room temperatures were below sixty degrees and gasoline was stringently rationed? This has produced a situation where militarily and psychologically Russia is the rising global power whereas the United States are the declining global power. That decline, camouflaged by *détente*, could be 'irreversible'. As President Nixon warned in a recent television address: 'What is at stake is whether the United States shall become the second strongest nation in the world.' But with the inheritance of the Vietnam disillusionment and the misery of Watergate, both of which are symptoms as much as causes, he has been fighting a rearguard action, less on the physical factors than on the factor of will.

The result might be only a temporary *détente* with Russia and a shattered alliance with western Europe. A temporary *détente* with the United States would suit the Russians very well and give them a free hand for the two important issues which inevitably loom ahead—the deaths of Chairman Mao in China and Marshal Tito in Yugoslavia. There cannot fail to be a struggle for the succession in both. In China, with the demise of Lin Piao, Russia would appear to have lost the pro-Moscow group which she would have backed for the succession, but she must be cultivating another and will make every effort, short of war,[67] to influence the result in her favour. In Yugoslavia there is likely to be fragmentation of the federal system with some parts being absorbed by communist neighbours[68] and the remainder being ruled by a pro-Moscow clique with Russian support. The end result, whether Yugoslavia is split into separate parts or held together by its army, will be its return to the Moscow fold and the provision of air and naval bases on the Adriatic coast for Russia. No one expects the United States to interfere in either country nor to have any influence on the result.

With regard to the shattered alliance, nearly five years ago I wrote that, in the short range, it would be the Russian aim to keep the West disunited, to erode and outflank NATO and to isolate the United States.[69] It is hardly necessary to read the newspapers in 1974 to see how well those objectives are being fulfilled, particularly after the Middle East war and the energy crisis. In continued pursuit of the final goal of winning World War III without a nuclear exchange, into which all this fits admirably, the Russian aim over the next few years must be to remove the United States' presence and influence entirely from the European, Asian and African land mass. That is by no means a preposterous step and, as in judo, it may require little exertion on the Russian part to engineer it, without risk of a confrontation. It is already working quite well in Australia.[70]

In an article on 'The Competitive Relationship' between the United States and the Soviet Union since World War II, Professor Zbigniew Brzezinski has drawn attention to its cyclical pattern with first one side being assertive and then the other. He attributes this swing in assertiveness to four major factors: the relative international standing, military power, economic power and the domestic policy base of the two countries. The United States, of course, has always had the advantage in economic power, although this has been much reduced by the wasteful consumption of their affluent society; the surplus is generally either eaten or burnt. In the other three factors, however, the advantage has varied at different periods since 1945. The Professor makes the point that the United States is only assertive when at least three, if not all four, factors are in its favour (1953–1957 and 1963–1968) whereas the Soviet Union has been prepared to be assertive with only one, or at the most two, factors in its favour (1948–1952, 1958–1963 and 1969–?). In this last period of Soviet Union assertiveness he has rated the international standing of the two powers as roughly equal, the military power as a questionably marginal United States advantage, economic power as still a United States advantage and the domestic policy base as a Soviet advantage. But in the year since the article was written we can see that the factor of international standing has definitely moved in favour of the Soviet Union, particularly as a reliable ally, and that military power is also clearly moving to the advantage of the Soviet Union. It may even be that Russia will obtain technological assistance, most favoured nation treatment in the United States, American trade credits and Japanese co-operation in the development of Siberia (all of which would be reasonable, judged on the merits of a package deal, if the other major factors were all still relatively favourable to the United States). If these are obtained, the gap in the economic power factor may begin to close and that in turn may increase the advantage in military power because of greater applied resources. This emphasizes one of the Professor's major points: 'Until now, the stability of the relationship has not been tested by an assertive Soviet policy conducted in the context of a clear Soviet military superiority.'

If South Vietnam falls because of a failure of American will, that test may come sooner rather than later. It could take the form of Hanoi tearing up the Ceasefire Agreement and launching another general offensive. This, if successful, might trigger further Arab moves, supported by Russia, either on oil or against Israel. By that time Israel might be in a position where its security depended entirely on an American guarantee. (A guarantee has only one meaning—the willingness to spill blood.) It is not difficult to visualize that there would be a panic-stricken attempt to get out of these obligations by talking. That would immediately indicate a readiness on the part of the United States to make all the concessions at the expense of its ally. This would herald such an American retreat, on a matter of vital national interest including good faith, that it would in the end invite confrontation at a time of complete Western disarray and of domestic vacillation within the United States. Instead of uniting, as in the past, everyone would run for cover. The stage would be set for strategic surrender.

Strategic surrender is not a subject which has received much attention. A book under that title was published in the late 1950s by Paul Kecskemeti for the Rand Corporation. It caused a minor furore at the time that a subject so alien to American thought could have been studied, and led to a debate in the Senate. Although the book was really a case history of the surrenders of France, Italy, Germany and Japan in World War II, Mr. Kecskemeti did make some rather prophetic statements to the effect that: 'Disaffected groups within a belligerent society often feel that it is the enemy's victory, rather than their own society's, that will bring their core values to fruition.' He added that: 'Extreme war weariness sometimes leads to such behaviour even in groups that were not disaffected at the outset.' That exactly describes the effect of the Vietnam war on American society and helps to prove a point (which I have maintained for many years) that it may turn out to be the decisive war of this century. Such disaffection will not be easily remedied and will surface on every occasion when the United States are faced with a critical issue. Facile slogans, such as 'No more Vietnams' or 'Bring America Home', may have precisely the opposite effect and bring it all, including the prospect of strategic surrender, home to America. That is the gravest danger facing the United States today.

The paragraph in Mr. Kecskemeti's book, which caused most of the trouble at the time, was one in which the possibility of an enemy obtaining a first strike capability leading to surrender without fighting was discussed, in order to show that surrender in such circumstances is a political act not dependent on a military decision. For the purpose of this book, however, I discount the possibility that such a first strike capability will be achieved by either side. I also discount a first strike without such a capability (for which there are many scenarios) which might require in response a counter-force capability against selected military targets to avoid, as the only option, massive retaliation against cities. But, after a major retreat on a matter of vital national interest which would leave in its wake a divided and vacillating society and doubtful allies, the fear of a nuclear exchange during confrontation might nullify all military capability and induce a strategic surrender, not just as a political act but as the only acceptable option.

There is still much to be learnt from a similar earlier context when there was 'a smell of burning' over the Cuban missile crisis in 1962. That was the closest that the world has yet come to a nuclear World War III since Russia became a nuclear power. One very important question about that episode has never been put nor answered. It will be remembered that, in the final year of President Eisenhower's administration, Vice-President Nixon had a very tough debate, known as 'the kitchen debate', with Mr. Khrushchev in Moscow and made it absolutely clear where he would stand on a number of world issues if elected as the next President in 1960. In the event, however, whether as a result of the cooking of Cook County or not, John Kennedy was elected President. In spite of his ringing inaugural address ('pay any price') Mr. Khrushchev gained a very low opinion of him after the Bay of Pigs affair[71] and after their summit meeting in Vienna in 1961. The question is: Would Khrushchev have put those missiles in Cuba if Nixon had been President? The answer is certainly No.

It is still a controversial matter whether the crisis was well handled or not. Khrushchev at least made two gains: the removal of American missiles from Turkey and, his primary objective, the safeguarding of the revolution in Cuba through an undertaking by the President never to invade Cuba. At least on the critical issue of the missiles in Cuba the President did not wobble. He was at that time in the fortunate position of having wide popular support in the United States, strong outside support, notably from Mr. Harold Macmillan then Prime Minister of the United Kingdom, and still an overwhelming nuclear superiority. In spite of all this he had allowed the United States — and this is the real criticism — to drift into a major confrontation for the simple reason that in the Soviet mind he lacked credibility.

Inheriting, as he did, the Vietnam war and the changed mood in the United States because of it, President Nixon four times during his tenure of office had to establish his own international credibility: the Cambodian operation in 1970; the mining of Haiphong in May, 1972; the B52 raids on Hanoi in December, 1972; and the alert of American forces during the Middle East war in October, 1973. He had none of President Kennedy's advantages — little popular support, almost no international support and a doubtful nuclear superiority — but his credibility was nevertheless established, at little risk and no great cost.[72] But in the poisoned atmosphere of Watergate, that credibility is waning and it is becoming doubtful whether any solid structure of world peace can be created and whether any succeeding Presidents in the next decade will restore that credibility, or create such a structure, unless they are very strong Presidents indeed.

The materials for that structure are all at hand and are contained in the four factors already mentioned: military power, sufficient in both the nuclear and conventional fields to maintain the deterrence; economic power, with all that it entails in the form of foreign aid, both for friends and sometimes foes; international standing, which requires a clear appreciation of vital interests, enforcement of agreements, and absolute faith with allies; and a supporting domestic policy base, for which will, nerve and stamina are the main ingredients.

The pillars of the structure, however, are geographical and rest in Europe, the Middle East, South East Asia and the Far East with their inter-connecting oceans. Fundamentally the United States, and the West, are maritime powers and are dependent on trade and the great sea lanes of history for their very existence.

But the question whether the United States will remain a great power, capable of holding the West together and of safeguarding (and bringing out the best in) western civilization, will depend less on the military, political and economic factors and more on the psychological factor which affects men's minds in every corner of the world. Unless the people of the United States understand that their credibility is at stake, and learn that the greater their credibility the less is the cost and the less the risk, it is going to be very dark indeed at the end of the tunnel.

NOTES

1. In *No Exit from Vietnam* I explained that the aim of insurgent strategy in protracted war was to reach a situation
   where the insurgents, at a cost that was indefinitely acceptable to themselves, were imposing costs on the government
   (and its allies) which were not indefinitely acceptable. At
   that point they must be winning. To counter this the
   threatened government must adopt a 'long haul low cost'
   strategy. This was designed to defeat the insurgency but
   at worst it might, where there were sanctuaries, produce a
   deadlock. I described such a deadlock later (in 1971) as
   'stable war' which, in my view, is better than 'no war no
   peace' because, if there is no peace, there must be some
   form of war.
2. They changed their surname to Nguyen, the most common
   surname in the South and that of the ruling family. In the
   same way, and possibly for the same symbolic reason (to
   identify himself with successful rebels), a later Nguyen
   (That Tan) changed his name finally to Ho (Chi Minh).
3. The Geneva Agreements are plural because separate
   military Agreements on the Cessation of Hostilities (i.e. a
   ceasefire) were signed on the one hand by a General of the
   People's Army of the DRV (North Vietman) and on the
   other by a Cambodian General in respect of Cambodia
   and by a French General in respect of both Laos and
   Vietnam. The South Vietnamese did not sign because their
   forces were technically included with those of France.
   Under the Agreement in respect of Vietnam the Vietminh
   were required to withdraw their forces north of the 17th
   Parallel and the French were required to withdraw their
   forces, including the South Vietnamese, south of it. The
   17th Parallel became the Demilitarized Zone (DMZ)
   which was about ten kilometres wide centred on the Ben
   Hai river.
4. The final Declaration represented a new departure in international diplomacy. Because it was not signed by any

members of the Conference, it did not have quite the same validity as the Agreements on Cessation of Hostilities. It was more than a hopeful communiqué drafted by the British and Russian Foreign Ministers, who were co-chairmen of the Conference, but its standing in international law has since been much disputed. Nevertheless, at the time, the American delegation and the South Vietnamese delegation (which was only an observer and not a member of the Conference), while expressing reservations about some of the Declaration's provisions, undertook not to disturb it by force. The Communist delegations gave no such undertaking.

5. See *Mandate for Change* by Dwight D. Eisenhower — Chapter XIV, *Chaos in Indochina* — published by Doubleday, New York, 1963.

6. As published and recorded in American Embassy summaries.

7. I accompanied the British Ambassador, Mr. John Moreton. An Independent Television News (ITN) camera team from London was also present and filmed the scene.

8. The only elections in South Vietnam since the ceasefire have been the mid-term elections for the Senate in August, 1973. The two government slates won with overwhelming majorities. The effect of this was that, later in the year, the GVN was able to obtain a two-thirds majority in a combined Senate and Lower House vote for an amendment to the constitution which would allow President Thieu to stand for further terms as President. Out of 219 members, 152 voted for the amendment thereby giving the government the necessary majority by six votes. This majority would not have been obtained if one of the small opposition parties (the 'Progressive Nationalists') with eight members had not voted with the government.

9. See the article by Professor Arnold Beichman on 'The Rise and Fall of the American Intellectual' in *Art International and the Lugano Review* of November, 1973, which makes the point that, while the intellectual always thinks he knows what is good for other people, the workers are perfectly capable of working this out for themselves. Sir Harold

Nicolson in his famous Diaries makes the same point on Munich—that the British working class knew appeasement was wrong.

10. See 'The Human Cost of Communism in Vietnam' prepared and published by the Committee on the Judiciary, United States Senate (U.S. Govt. Printing Office, 1972, No. 72–241 0) which contains on pp 34–44 a paper by Miss Anita Nutt on reprisals, the ICC and other matters. The land reform pogrom alone after 1954 is estimated to have accounted for 100,000 killed.

11. Ibid. p. 101, from report in *Washington Daily News,* 25 Nov. '69.

12. See *The Military Balance 1973–1974* published by the International Institute for Strategic Studies, 18 Adam Street, London W.C.2. Only Russia and China have more than the combined total for both Vietnams. India, North and South Korea and Taiwan are close.

13. A plaque in the Hoare Memorial Hall, Church House, Westminster, reads: THIS HALL OF CHURCH HOUSE WAS AS OCCASION REQUIRED DURING THE YEARS 1940, 1941 and 1944 THE CHAMBER OF THE HOUSE OF COMMONS. WITHIN ITS WALLS, THE PRIME MINISTER, WINSTON CHURCHILL, IN THE DARKEST DAYS OF THE WAR SPOKE TO THE COMMONS AND TO THE NATION THE WORDS HERE RECORDED: 'Today, inaugurated in the session of Parliament, we proclaim the depth and sincerity of our resolve to keep vital and active, even in the midst of our struggle for life, even under the fire of the enemy, those Parliamentary institutions which have served us so well, and have proved themselves the most flexible institutions for securing ordered unceasing change and progress; which, while they throw open the portals of the future, carry forward also the traditions and glories of the past, and at this solemn moment in the world's history are at once the broadest assertion of a British freedom and the expression of an unconquerable national will.'

14. *The Village* by F. J. West, Jr., published by Harper and Row, New York, 1972.

15. *Times Literary Supplement* of 12 January, 1973.

16. Published in *Aftenposten*, Oslo, 11 September, 1973.
17. Article in *Foreign Affairs* of January, 1969.
18. His name was Ho Huu Cong of Long Truong hamlet, Long Tri village, Binh Phuoc district in Long An province, if you want to check it. But there were thousands of similar cases, all on record.
19. Already quoted — see note 10. The few critics who attempted to dispute it could only do so by calling it 'hysterical', a favourite means of disparaging an uncomfortable argument.
20. An American friend told me that, after the Tet offensive had been shown on TV, it was impossible to convince a student audience that there was a building left standing in Saigon. Similarly, at the end of 1969 an English audience was surprised when I showed slides taken that year of the Mekong Delta showing thousands and thousands of acres of billowing rice fields when they had expected to see a lunar landscape.
21. See *North Vietnam's Blitzkrieg — an Interim Assessment* — Conflict Study No. 27 by Ian Ward of the London *Daily Telegraph,* produced for the Institute for the Study of Conflict, 17 Northumberland Avenue, London W.C.2. 'La Route Terrible' runs parallel to 'Street Without Joy' (in the Vietminh war against the French) made famous by the late Bernard Fall's book.
22. In this highest figure of 39,790, the normal criminal element was higher than one-third at over 17,000, while the two communist elements were just under 22,500. I am convinced of the accuracy of these figures because there was not the accommodation for more and no further groups could have been hidden from the very close official American scrutiny at a time when Americans in large numbers were still serving down to District level. Moreover the GVN had no reason to exclude any such groups from the categories stated. This does not mean that a few individuals, but only a few, may not have been excluded.
23. For example, American POWs held by Hanoi and Israeli prisoners held by Syria.
24. See *Five Years to Freedom* by James N. Rowe, published by Little, Brown & Co., Boston, 1971. James Rowe was a prisoner of the Vietcong in the U Minh forest area for five

years and managed to escape. This is not a book for the squeamish.

25. Hearings on U.S. Assistance Programs in Vietnam before a subcommittee of the Committee on Government Operations, House of Representatives, July 15, 16, 19, 21, and August 2, 1971. The figures quoted later for incidents, casualties and claims relating to the Phoenix programme are from the same hearings.

26. Readers may note that these both occurred in one week in one Military Region (I). I had merely asked at that time for two or three examples. Any other week and any other Region would probably have produced similar incidents.

27. See *Time* of 18 May, 1970, and for a fuller account *Kissinger — The Uses of Power* by David Landau, published by Houghton Mifflen, 1972 — pp. 94–102.

28. *Newsweek* of 1 January, 1968, one month before the Tet offensive, contained some euphoric statements. My own small contribution to the effect that 'you are not winning' struck a rather discordant note, but elicited an invitation to go and see for myself. When I arrived during the offensive the question was: 'What went wrong?'

29. *No Exit from Vietnam* published by Chatto and Windus, London, and David McKay Co. Inc., New York, 1969.

30. See David Holden in the London *Sunday Times* of 6 May, 1973.

31. See Documents relating to British involvement in the Indochina conflict 1945–65, H M Stationery Office, Cmnd. 2834, December, 1965. One paragraph of this I C C report reads: 'Having examined the complaints and the supporting material sent by the South Vietnamese Mission, the Committee has come to the conclusion that in specific instances there is evidence to show that armed and unarmed personnel, arms, munitions and other supplies have been sent from the Zone in the North to the Zone in the South with the object of supporting, organizing and carrying out hostile activities, including armed attacks, directed against the Armed Forces and Administration of the Zone in the South. These acts are in violation of Articles 10, 19, 24, and 27 of the Agreement on the Cessation of Hostilities in Viet-Nam.'

32. For example, supplies to NVA 1 Division were going from Kratie to south of Kampong Thom, across the Ton Le Sap north of Phnom Penh, through the foothills of the Kirikoms to the South Vietnamese border between Ha Tien and Chau Duc—a distance of about 250 miles.

33. He was commanding General, U.S. Military Assistance Command, Vietnam, from 1968 until he became Chief of Staff, U.S. Army, at the end of 1972.

34. Later Brigadier-General, commanding the 2nd Division, responsible for recapturing Sa Huynh in the ceasefire fighting.

35. He was killed on 9 June, 1972, in a helicopter crash flying into Kontum at night and was awarded the Medal of Freedom. A biography of this outstanding American is being written by Neil Sheehan of the *New York Times*.

36. John Vann's rescue of the American Advisory Team in a night helicopter operation was an epic of courage and determination in the face of intense enemy fire.

37. Since Dien Bien Phu there has been a tendency to give General Vo Nguyen Giap the credit for the whole strategy of the war. But we shall never really know how much was due to him or to his senior colleagues on the Politburo, all of whom had equivalent experience of this type of war. It is likely that Giap's contribution (and brilliance) has been overrated and that the major decisions were made by others or jointly. Giap has certainly been a great believer in artillery as the key to victory.

38. Already mentioned in Chapter III—see note 21.

39. The Senators were not alone. An article in *Worldview* of October, 1972, for example, condemned the bombing as useless and immoral. It also argued that the GVN was corrupt, dictatorial and incompetent; that Pacification was a failure and Vietnamization a farce. It failed to explain why, in that case, the NVA had been unable to capture and hold any province capital and only half a dozen district towns out of 268, and why Hanoi was offering ceasefire terms which it had previously rejected.

40. By August of 1972, 14 communist divisions and 26 independent regiments were in South Vietnam. Six communist

divisions operated in northern Military Region (MR) I—
the 304th, 308th, major elements of the 312th, 320B, 324B,
and 325th. In southern MR I there was an *ad hoc* division—
the 711th—formed from several independent regiments in
the area. Another division, the 2nd, also operated in
southern MR I, having moved from MR II in June and
July. The 320th and 3rd Divisions were in MR II. MR III
had the 7th and 9th Divisions; while the 5th Division and
elements of the 1st Division were in Region IV or Cambodia. This left one division, the 316th, and 4 independent
regiments in Laos. There were not known to be any regular
forces (except Navy, Air Force and AA) left in North
Vietnam at all.

41. *No Exit from Vietnam*—Chapter VI.

42. I had thought that the release of fifty might have created an
    uncontrollable emotional avalanche within the United
    States but I now realize, as Hanoi did, that it could have had
    the opposite effect. Quite apart from revealing the brutal
    treatment of POWs, too many of the fifty would have called
    on the United States to renew and increase the bombing and
    to keep the pressure up.

43. The quotations from Alexander Solzhenitsyn in this and the
    last two chapters are taken from his *Open Letter to the Soviet
    Leaders*, published in the London *Sunday Times*, 3 March,
    1974.

44. Issued by the United States Information Service—presum-
    ably a tape recording.

45. See the analysis in *The Aviation Week and Space Technology
    Magazine* of 1 January, 1973, and subsequent issues.

46. The books by POWs on their treatment and on this point are
    just beginning to come out.

47. The Provisional Revolutionary Government (Vietcong) was
    only able to raise about one-third of the allocated members
    on this Commission. It was one indication of how weak the
    Vietcong were militarily.

48. One South Vietnamese outpost, Tong Le Chan, not far
    from An Loc, was besieged by the NVA for over 400 days
    and finally fell in April, 1974. Because of intense NVA fire
    it could not be supplied except by parachute drop and

there was no means of relieving the small garrison of little more than a company without large-scale operations. A number of outposts such as these were 'in-place' at the time of the ceasefire and the GVN had every right to maintain them under the agreement.

49. The whole subject of rear bases and sanctuaries requires much more study, not only with regard to the Vietnam war. In my view there are three principal aims in making war: to defeat the enemy's main forces in the field; to disrupt his rear bases; and to break his will to resist or to attack. Americans tend to jump from the first to the third without paying too much attention to the second, either in defence or attack. In conditions of 'limited' war this leads to allies of the United States being forced into can-lose can't-win situations (see Chapter X), because their rear bases continue to be threatened while the other side's rear bases are not. Note, for example, how the Ceasefire Agreement of January, 1973, in Vietnam restored the security of North Vietnam's rear bases in North Vietnam, Laos and Cambodia while the South's rear base in South Vietnam remained subject to military attack. The same may occur with Israel.

50. The increase over the decade was 111 per cent. In 1973 imports, measured in real terms and allowing for price inflation, were 24 per cent below the 1969 level and 14 per cent below the high point reached in 1966. The annual average rate of increase of 7·8 per cent is almost certainly an overestimate, because the International Monetary Fund indices on which it is based do not adequately reflect the price increases in those commodities on which South Vietnam has been particularly dependent—gasoline, fertilizer, rice and sugar.

51. Much play has been made of the fact that four F 5As were replaced by four F 5Es, which are a much improved version. Even if this offended the clause in the Ceasefire Agreement which required that replacements should be of equivalent characteristics, it bore no comparison with, for example, the installation of sixteen SAMs at Khe Sanh and the building of an airstrip there for MIG 21s (quite

apart from any other infringements with regard to tanks and heavy guns introduced by the NVA, some of which themselves may be improved versions).

52. If the same definition of 'political prisoner', as was applied to Vietnam, was applied to the United States, then the whole prison population there would be political prisoners including, for example, the assassin of Senator Robert Kennedy (who might be so defined). My own definition of a political prisoner would be someone who is not a POW and who is detained without having committed a criminal offence against the laws of the country, or without being brought to trial for that offence for political reasons.

53. At the end of the Emergency in Malaya in 1960 about 500 remaining insurgents under Chin Peng took refuge on the Thai border. Their numbers have now been built up to about 2,000 and small units have been penetrating down the central mountain chain in Malaya to a depth of 60–70 miles.

54. Burma.

55. As Professor Max Beloff wrote in an article on fellow-travellers *(Daily Telegraph*, London, 18 January, 1973): 'After all, the test of a "front" organization is a very clear one: does it fight evils in general; wars, political persecution, or whatever it may be, or does it only combat wars waged by the United States and its allies, political persecutions only of the Left by the Right and never vice versa?'

56. The best example is the carving up of Poland by Russia and Germany in 1939, but in Argentina the Left happily backed the return of President Peron to the Presidency.

57. From the Foreword to *The Art of Counter-Revolutionary War* by John J. McCuen, published by Faber and Faber Ltd., London, 1966.

58. North Atlantic Treaty Organization, Central Treaty Organization (including Turkey and Iran) and South East Asia Treaty Organization.

59. It has been generally assumed that only the United States learnt tactical and technological lessons from the Vietnam war, but Russia learnt plenty too, which were put to good

use in the Middle East war of 1973: for example, the strategic mobility provided by naval and air transport forces, missile defence against a tactical air force, the tactical use of helicopters, the advantage of direction over advice, and much improved weaponry and electronic devices.

60. It was reported that about 500,000 communists were slaughtered mainly as a result of a popular uprising against them. The Army did nothing to stop it owing to the bestial treatment accorded to ten or more generals who were captured by the communists during the attempted coup and were then tortured and cut into small pieces by hepped-up female cadres.

61. The figures quoted are from *The Military Balance 1973–1974* — See note 12.

62. See two special studies produced by the Institute for the Study of Conflict in March, 1974 — *Soviet Objectives in the Middle East* and *The Security of the Cape Oil Route*.

63. See *Gunboat Diplomacy* by James Cable, published for the International Institute for Strategic Studies by Chatto and Windus, London, 1971.

64. From *Revolutionary War in World Strategy, 1945–1969.*

65. The best comment so far published on 'guerrilla diplomacy' is contained in *Indo-China: The Conflict Analysed* by Dennis J. Duncanson (Conflict Studies, No. 39), published by The Institute for the Study of Conflict, October, 1973.

66. When on 6 May, 1974, Senator Edward Kennedy's amendment to a military supplementary aid bill — to cut $266 millions for South Vietnam — was passed by the Senate by 43 votes to 38, it signified that perhaps the major lesson of the Vietnam war is: do not rely on the United States as an ally. This vote may prove to be one of the initial steps leading to the strategic surrender of the United States. 6 May, 1974, may therefore become an important historical date.

67. I say 'short of war' because it is acknowledged that China now has the nuclear capability to inflict unacceptable damage on Russia.

68. Bulgaria has long coveted Macedonia, but the fur would really fly if Albania, supported by China, was to claim the

province of Kosova (inhabited mainly by Albanians) with Russia supporting its retention by Yugoslavia.

69. From *Revolutionary War in World Strategy*.

70. Under the Labour government of Prime Minister Gough Whitlam, but this will depend on the result of the General Election called for 18 May, 1974. He just won it.

71. An abortive attempt to invade Cuba with a force composed mainly of Cuban refugees.

72. It would be interesting to speculate how the Vietnam war would have gone if Richard Nixon had become President in 1960. It certainly would not have followed the same course and might have been successfully concluded by 1964.

INDEX

Abrams, Creighton, Gen., 73, 98, 112
Agreement on the Cessation of Hostilities in Vietnam *see* Geneva Agreements
Amnesty International, 153
An Loc, battle for, 41, 100, 106–110
Army of the Republic of Vietnam (ARVN), popular support for, 40; equipment, 63, 64, 66; and Cambodia operations, 78, 87, 146; and US withdrawal, 79; effectiveness, 91, 92, 107, 110–112, 155, 169; and 1972 invasion, 96–99, 102–112; and ceasefire violations, 142, 144
Association of South East Asian Nations (ASEAN), 121

Ba, Brig-Gen., 105–6
Bao Dai, 8
Beichman, Arnold, 192
Beloff, Max, 199
Brezhnev, Leonid, 115, 176, 184
British Advisory Mission, 34, 35
Brzezinski, Zbigniew, 185–186
Bui Cong Tuong, 70
Bunker, Ellsworth, 164

Cable, James, 200
Cai Be (village), 39
Cambodia (Khmer Republic), and Vietminh, 7; under Sihanouk, 30; refugees from, 42; as Vietcong operational base, 50; and North's war aims, 59; North's activities and presence, 74–76, 84, 88, 96, 114, 123, 159; operations in, 76–78, 85, 87, 123, 146; and 1972 invasion, 97, 99; and peace negotiations, 118, 125, 138, 173; neutrality violated, 140, 146; war in, 146–151; US bombing, 147–149, 154; communication, 167; and Geneva Agreements, 191
Castro, Fidel, 172, 176

Ceasefire Agreements: January 1973, 136, 137, 198; June 1973 ('Joint Communiqué'), 53, 124, 128, 129, 182
Cham Empire, 5
Chau, Tran Ngoc *see* Tran Ngoc Chau
Chieu, Tran Van *see* Tran Van Chieu
Chin Peng, 199
China, influence on Vietnam, 2, 3, 6, 23; and Russia, 23, 93, 94, 154, 177, 185, 200; killings in, 25; US opposition to, 27, 28; nuclear tests, 37; support for North, 89, 92, 154, 163; and peace negotiations, 126; and Sihanouk, 146; relations with US, 154; and Africa, 180; nuclear capability, 200
Chinh, Truong *see* Truong Chinh
Churchill, Winston S., 12, 16, 33, 179, 193
Chuyen, Le Xuyen *see* Le Xuyen Chuyen
Clark, Ramsey, 36
Clausewitz, Carl von, 169
Clifford, Clark, 79
Colby, William, 49
Con Son island, 53
Concerned Asia Scholars, Committee of, 32, 72
Conquest, Robert, 35
Cuba, 177, 188, 201

Dac, Tran Van *see* Tran Van Dac
Davison, Mike, Lt.-Gen., 76
detention *see* prisoners
Diem, Ngo Dinh, President *see* Ngo Dinh Diem
Do, Tran Van *see* Tran Van Do
Dong, Pham Van *see* Pham Van Dong
Duan, Le *see* Le Duan
Duncanson, Dennis J., 200

203